Introduction

By making your training units more diverse, you can increase the players' motivation, since you consistently offer new approaches to improve and refine familiar movement sequences. In this book, you will find inspiring exercises you can apply during each phase of your everyday team handball training – from warm-up and goalkeeper warm-up shooting to the common contents of the main phase and the closing games. Each exercise is illustrated and described in an easy, comprehensible manner. Specific notes give you tips on what you need to be aware of.

This book deals with the following key subjects:

Warm-up:
- Basic warm-up
- Short warm-up games
- Sprint contests
- Coordination
- Ball familiarization
- Goalkeeper warm-up shooting

Basic exercises, basic play, and target play:
- Offense/series of shots
- General offense
- Fast throw-off
- 1st and 2nd wave
- Defensive action
- Closing games
- Endurance

At the end of this book, you will find an entire methodological training unit. The objective of this training unit is to improve shooting and quick decision-making under pressure.

This reference book contains 75 individual exercises.

Sample figure:

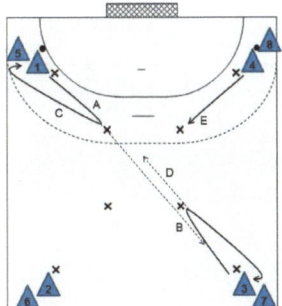

Dynamic group piston movement

1st English edition released on 19 Feb 2016
German original edition released on 19 Feb 2015

Published by DV Concept
Editors, Design and Layout: Jörg Madinger, Elke Lackner
Proofreading and English translation: Nina-Maria Nahlenz

ISBN: 978-3-95641-164-9

The book and its contents are protected by copyright. No reprinting, photomechanical reproduction, storing or processing in electronic systems without the publisher's written permission.

Contents:
1. Basic warm-up

No.	Name	Difficulty level
1	Team pursuit	★
2	Warm-up with the ball and easy shooting at the goal	★
3	Passing from player to player with additional running exercises	★
4	Blindfolded warm-up	★
5	Warm-up with subsequent shooting on targets	★

2. Short warm-up games

6	Taking down the vaulting box by shooting	★
7	Team ball in three squares	★
8	Team ball with subsequent action	★★
9	Team ball with two different tasks	★★★
10	2-on-2 intensive soccer variant	★★

3. Sprint contests

11	Sprint relay race with balance benches	★
12	Going to Jerusalem	★
13	Team tag	★★
14	Intensive sprint competition	★★★
15	Sprint competition with playing cards	★★

4. Coordination

16	Sprint reaction with numbers	★
17	Coordination reactions	★
18	Coordination run with defensive action	★
19	Coordination run	★★
20	Ball coordination with five balls	★★★

5. Ball familiarization

21	Pass and run at signal	★
22	Pass and catch across the whole court in groups of 2	★
23	Dynamic group piston movement	★★
24	Running feint with subsequent catch and pass in full speed	★★
25	Pass and catch across the whole court with goalkeeper	★★

6. Goalkeeper warm-up shooting

26	Running exercise with subsequent shot	★
27	Two-position warm-up shooting	★★
28	Dynamic warm-up shooting with subsequent fast break initiation	★★
29	Warm-up shooting with defense exercise	★★
30	"Intelligent" warm-up shooting (on instruction) with subsequent fast break	★★

7. Offense/series of shots

31	Simple series of shots with coordination run	★
32	Series of shots on instruction	★
33	Series of shots with extended coordination run	★★
34	Complex all-position series of shots	★★★
35	Intensive series of shots after previous exertion	★★★

8. General offense

No.	Name	Difficulty level
36	Back and forth (piston) movement with subsequent wing player shot	★
37	2-on-2 team play with additional exercises	★
38	Simple crossing with decision-making: RB/LB and wing player	★★
39	Simple crossing with continued playing: CB and wing player	★★
40	Russian screen in the HL/HR positions – Initiation	★★
41	Russian screen in the HL/HR positions – Subsequent action	★★
42	3-on-3 simple crossing	★★

9. Fast throw-off/1st and 2nd wave

No.	Name	Difficulty level
43	Fast throw-off	★★
44	Coordination legwork with two subsequent 1-on-1 fast break situations	★★
45	Quick running moves with subsequent 1-on-1 fast break	★★
46	2nd wave – Initiation	★★
47	Fast break competition	★★

10. Defensive action

No.	Name	Difficulty level
48	Stealing the ball	★
49	Basic practice: Step out and secure	★
50	1-on-1 play with subsequent action for the attacking player	★
51	1-on-1 offense and defense switching	★★
52	Intensive continuous defense and offense switching with subsequent action	★★★
53	Intensive continuous 1-on-1 defense and offense play after previous exertion	★★★
54	2-on-2 continuous defense switching with additional exercise	★★
55	Middle block pivot hand-over and take-over	★★
56	Goal corner switching between defense players and goalkeeper	★★★
57	Outnumbered middle block defense	★★
58	4-on-4 defensive action with subsequent fast break on the wing positions	★★

11. Closing games

No.	Name	Difficulty level
59	4-on-4 with quick offense/defense switching	★★
60	Fast throw-off and 2nd wave switch game	★★
61	Simple 4-on-4 switch game	★
62	Intensive 4-on-4 switch game	★★

12. Endurance

No.	Name	Difficulty level
63	Piston movement and passing with additional running paths and under time pressure	★
64	Ball familiarization exercise focusing on running	★★
65	Outdoor endurance competition on the cinder tracks	★★
66	Continuous fast break with subsequent athletics course	★★★
67	Running with additional exercise on the large safety mat	★★★

13. Example training unit no. 220 "Shooting improvement and quick decision-making under pressure"

14. Editor's note

15. Other reference books published by DV Concept

From warm-up to handball team play
75 exercises for every handball training

Key:

No. of exercise — Name of exercise — Minimum number of players

No. 1	Team pursuit	8	★
Topic:	General warm-up		
Equipment required:	Sufficient number of handballs		

Difficulty level
Easy: ★
Medium: ★★
Difficult: ★★★

✗ Cone

◯ Hoop

Large safety mat

Small gym mat

Small vaulting box

Small vaulting box, upside down

Foam noodles: foam bars of approx. 60 cm length

Large vaulting box

Medicine ball

Soft ball/tennis ball

Balance bench

Hurdle

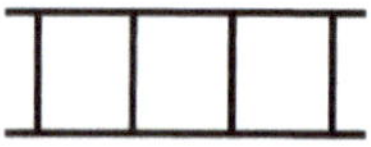

Coordination ladder

Bibs in different colors

1. Basic warm-up

No. 1	Team pursuit	8	★
	Topic:	General warm-up		
	Equipment required:	Sufficient number of handballs		

Basic setting:
- Divide the team into groups of 4 or 5 players and determine the leader of each group.

Course:
- The groups move freely across the court.
- The leader runs ahead and shows exercises. The other players follow and copy the leader's exercises (A).
- If two groups meet and the leaders exchange high fives, the following players need to switch their leaders. They must react immediately and copy the new leader's exercises.
- Once the coach whistles, another player becomes the leader and must show exercises at once.
- And so on.

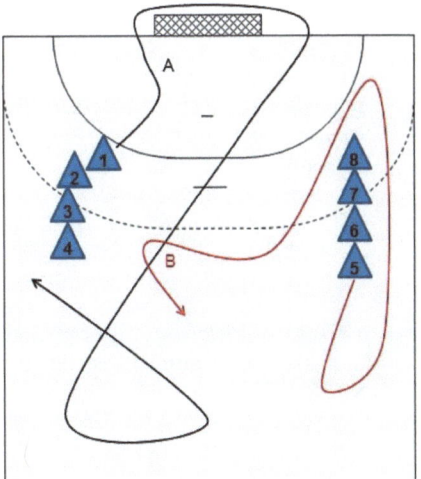

Variant:
- Each player has a handball.

No. 2	Warm-up with the ball and easy shooting at the goal	6	★
Topic:	General warm-up		
Equipment required:	One handball per player		

Course:
- The players crisscross throughout one half of the court and dribble one handball each (A).
- The players need to perform different running and dribbling variants (such as dribbling with the throwing hand, dribbling with the non-throwing hand, dribbling with both hands alternately; hopping, sidestepping, running backwards, etc.)
- Once the coach whistles, the players try to throw their handball into the goal from their current position (B).
- Afterwards, the players fetch their handballs and start dribbling again.

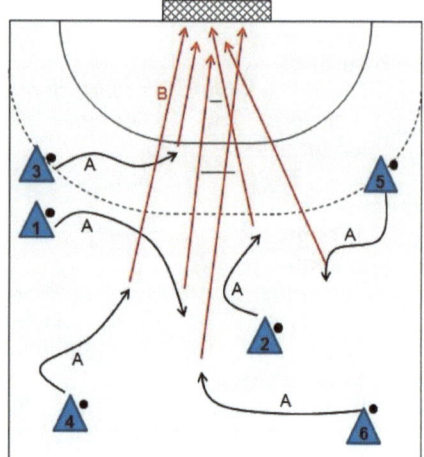

No. 3	Passing from player to player with additional running exercises	8	★
	Topic: General warm-up		
Equipment required:	2 handballs		

Course 1:
- The team is divided into two groups. The players of each group are given numbers (figure: 1 to 5).
- The players crisscross throughout the court at relaxed pace.
- Each group passes a handball (A and B) according to the predefined order (1-2-3-4-5-1 etc.).
- Following each pass, the player who passed the ball sprints to one of the side lines (C) and then crisscrosses throughout the court again at a relaxed pace until he receives the next pass.
- The players may choose a side line for their sprint; however, they are not allowed to choose the line that is closest (D).

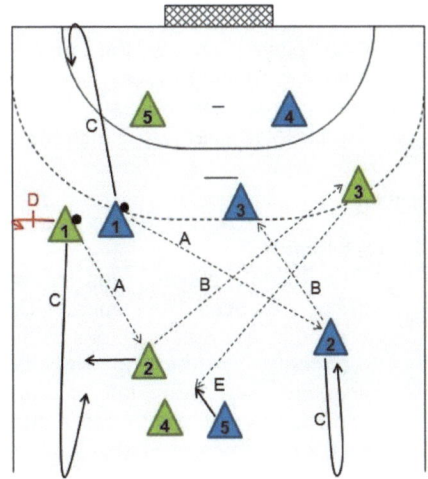

Course 2:
- The course remains the same as course 1.
- Additionally, the players of the opposing team who are currently not involved in passing or sprinting to one of the side lines are now allowed to steal the other group's ball (E).

Variant:
- The players need to perform different running variants (hopping, sidestepping, arm rotation).

No. 4	Blindfolded warm-up	6	★
	Topic:	General warm-up	
	Equipment required:	Sufficient number of colored bibs, blindfolds for each pair of players	

Course 1:
- The players form pairs.
- One player shows the running path and running moves, the other player copies the moves.
- Switch roles after 2 to 3 minutes.

Course 2:
- One of the two players is wearing a blindfold.
- The "blind" player runs ahead swiftly across the court. The second player guides his teammate by touching him (left shoulder → turn left / right shoulder → turn right / soft patting on the back → stop) (A).
- Switch roles after 2 to 3 minutes.

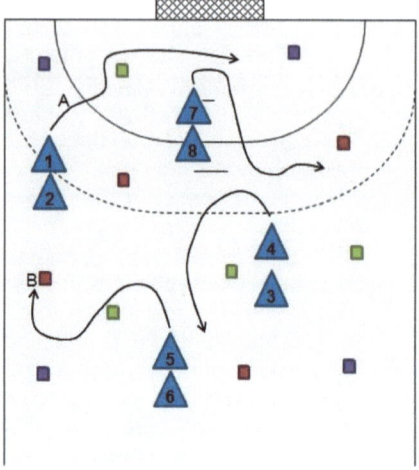

Course 3 (figure):
- Put some objects (e.g., colored bibs) on the court floor.
- The players perform course 2 and try to collect as many objects as possible (B).
- Only the "blind" player is allowed to pick up the objects (sign: patting on both shoulders).
- Switch roles after 2 to 3 minutes.

⚠ The players should run across the court at pace, even though they are blindfolded; they must trust their teammate.

⚠ The players are not allowed to talk during the exercise.

No. 5	Warm-up with subsequent shooting on targets	6	★
	Topic: General warm-up		
Equipment required:	Different balls (e.g., handballs, soft balls, tennis balls), 1 balance bench, 5 cones		

Setting (see figure):
- Put different balls (handballs, soft balls, tennis balls, etc.) on the floor of one half of the court.
- Put a balance bench into the goal zone and place cones on top.

Course:
- The players move swiftly around the balls throughout the entire half of the court (A). They are not allowed to enter the goal zone. They perform different running variants.
- Once the coach whistles, each player fetches a ball (B), runs to the 6-meter line (C), and tries to shoot a cone (D).
- After throwing, the players fetch the remaining balls and shoot until no cone is left or until all balls have been thrown into the goal zone.
- The players then start to run again while the coach prepares the next shooting sequence (distribution of balls on the floor in one half of the court) and then, once again, gives the sign for shooting.

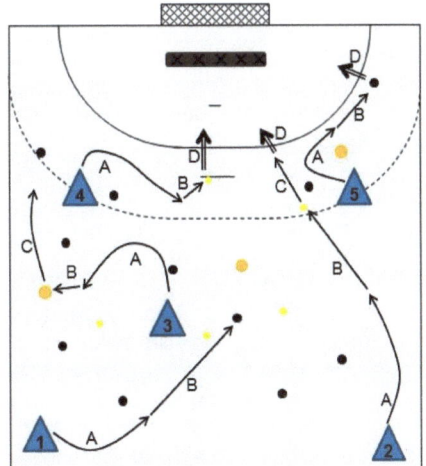

⚠ Vary the distance between the shooting line and the bench, i.e. adjust to the players' level of performance.

⚠ Each player is only allowed to pick up one ball at a time in order to shoot.

⚠ The players are not allowed to pass the balls; they need to shoot with the ball they picked up themselves.

2. Short warm-up games

No. 6	Taking down the vaulting box by shooting	8	★
	Topic: Short warm-up games		
	Equipment required: Two large vaulting boxes, 1 handball, 6 cones		

Setting:
- Position two large vaulting boxes diagonally and use cones to define the shooting line.

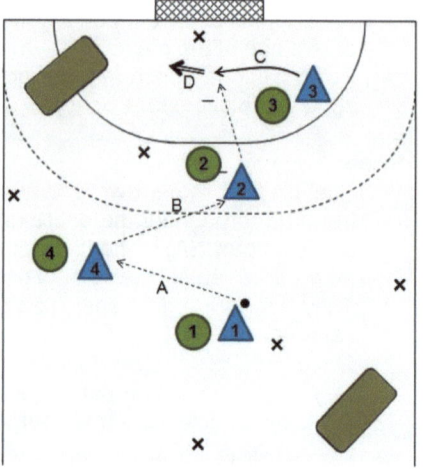

Course:
- Two teams play against each other.
- By passing quickly (A and B) and moving in a well-coordinated manner (C), the attacking team tries to put a player in a good shooting position (D).
- The team scores if the shooting player hits one side of the vaulting box.
- The shooting player is not allowed to step into the defined area around the vaulting box.
- Following each shooting attempt, the other team gets the ball and starts an attack on the opposite vaulting box.
- As soon as one of the teams has scored two (three) times, remove one of the intermediate parts of the vaulting box.
- The team that takes down their vaulting box first wins the game.

⚠ Following a shooting attempt, the players need to adjust immediately and start an attack on the opposite vaulting box.

No. 7	Team ball in three squares	8	★
	Topic: Short warm-up games		
	Equipment required: 3 different throwing toys, e.g., 1 handball, 1 frisbee, 1 softball; 8 cones		

Setting:
- Define three playing fields using cones and make two teams.
- Both teams play team ball on the individual playing fields using the respective throwing toy. The players are not allowed to bounce the toy.
- Choose a different throwing toy for each playing field, e.g., common handball, medicine ball, frisbee, soft ball, tennis ball, etc.
- After playing, the throwing toys must remain in the respective playing field.

Course:
- The team in possession of the toy tries to pass it 8 times (return passes are not allowed).
- If the opposing team steals the toy, they may immediately try to pass it 8 times.
- The team scores, if they manage to pass the toy 8 times. After scoring, the toy must be put on the floor at once.
- Now the coach whistles once or twice, which is the sign for both teams to change the playing field accordingly.

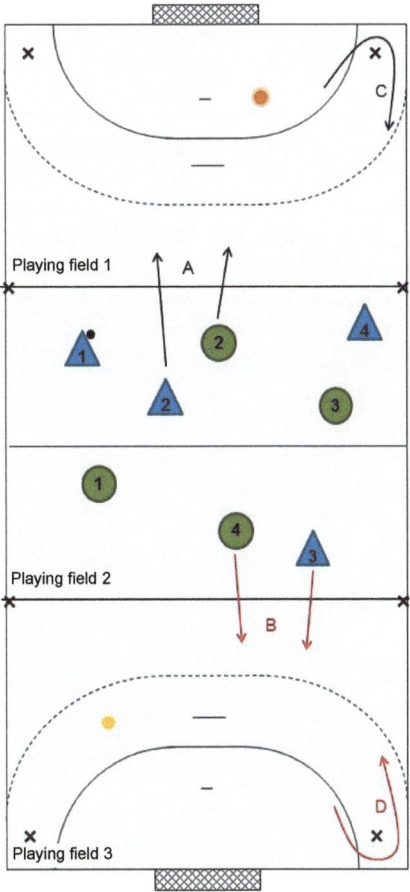

Changing the playing field upon the coach's whistle:
- One whistle: Change playing field upwards (A).
- Two whistles: Change playing field downwards (B).
- The team that first secures the new throwing toy may immediately try to pass it 8 times.

Examples:
- End of game on playing field 1
    - One whistle; the players need to move to playing field 3. However, the players need to sprint around one of the two cones first before they are allowed to enter playing field 3 (C).
    - Two whistles; the players need to move to playing field 2.
- End of game on playing field 2
    - One whistle; the players need to move to playing field 1.
    - Two whistles; the players need to move to playing field 3.
- End of game on playing field 3
    - One whistle; the players need to move to playing field 2.
    - Two whistles; the players need to move to playing field 1. However, the players need to sprint around one of the two cones first before they are allowed to enter playing field 1 (D).

⚠ If the teams remain in one playing field for too long, due to constantly switching ball possession, the coach may whistle anytime in between. The players need to adjust to the new situation immediately.

No. 8	Team ball with subsequent action	8	★★
	Topic: Short warm-up games		
Equipment required:	1 handball, 8 to 10 cones		

Setting:
- Use cones to define several goals.
- Assign the numbers 1 to 4 to the side lines.
- Make two teams.

Course:
- The teams play against each other.
- By running and passing the ball in a well-coordinated manner (A), the team in ball possession tries to pass the ball 5 (3, 7) times to a teammate by bouncing it through one of the defined goals (B or D).
- The players must attack a different goal each time (C). They are not allowed to bounce the ball through the same goal two times in a row.
- The attacking team counts the bouncing passes through the goals aloud.
- As soon as the team has passed the ball through the cones 5 times, the coach calls out a number between 1 and 4 (E).
- The attacking team now tries to lay down the ball behind the respective side line (F).
- The team scores if they manage to complete the whole course (pass 5 times through a goal and subsequently lay down the ball behind the correct side line).
- The other team fetches the ball and now tries to score as well.
- If there is a switch in ball possession, the goal counting starts over from 1.

⚠️ The players need to switch quickly and run to the next goal immediately after scoring. After the team has passed the ball through the cones 5 times, the players need to run to the respective side line at once.

⚠️ As soon as the scoring team has laid down the ball behind the side line, the other team needs to fetch the ball immediately and start an attack on the goals.

No. 9	Team ball with two different tasks	10	★★★
	Topic: Short warm-up games		
Equipment required:	1 handball, 8 small gym mats, 4 cones		

Course:
- Both teams play team ball within the defined playing field (cones); however, they are not allowed to dribble. If a team manages to pass 8 times in a row, without the other team stealing the ball, the second part of the game begins.
- The attacking players now try to pass the ball to a teammate standing on one of the gym mats (C). If the player on the mat catches the ball, the team scores and stays in possession of the ball. In order to score again however, the team needs to attack a different gym mat.
- The team does not score if there is an opponent standing on the same gym mat as the attacking player while this player catches the ball (A).
- The players keep playing until the ball gets lost. The teams need to count the score (times they caught the ball while standing on a gym mat) themselves.
- Which team manages to catch the ball on the gym mat most often and scores highest?

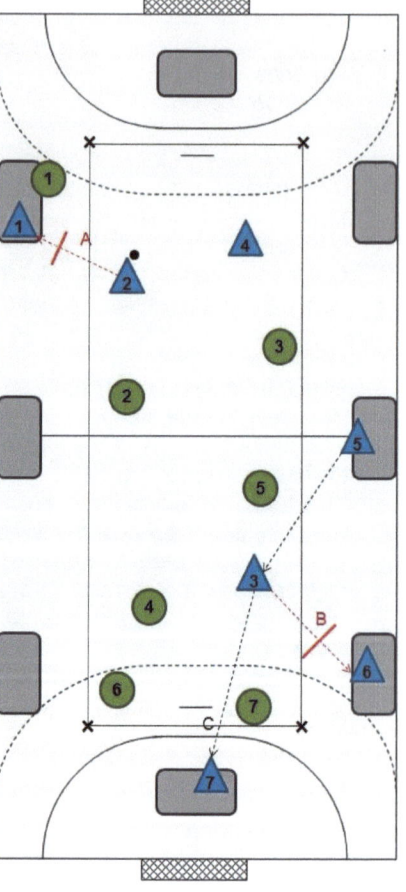

Variants:
- Only a maximum of 3 players per team are allowed in the outer playing field (around the gym mats).
- After scoring, the players are neither allowed to attack the same gym mat again nor to attack the neighboring mats (B).

No. 10	**2-on-2 intensive soccer variant**	12	★★
	Topic: Short warm-up games		
	Equipment required: 1 soccer ball, 4 balance benches		

Setting:
- Position four balance benches as shown in the figure. The seating surfaces must point towards the court (turned over by 90 degrees).
- Make two teams.
- The teams play soccer 2-on-2.
- The teams need to decide in which order their players are to enter the playing field.

Course:
- 🔺1 and 🔺2 play against 🟢1 and 🟢2 and try to score by kicking the ball against the seating surface of the balance bench (A, B, and C).
- If a team scores, the four players 🔺1, 🔺2, 🟢1, and 🟢2 need to leave the playing field at their balance bench immediately (D) (give a high-five). They are not allowed to enter the game again while leaving the playing field. One new player per balance bench is allowed to enter the playing field then (E).
- Now, 🔺3 and 🔺5 play against 🟢3 and 🟢5 until a team scores the next goal. The players then also leave the playing field at their balance bench, and so on.
- The players waiting outside to be substituted do both push-ups and sit-ups alternately during the waiting periods.

⚠️ For larger groups, play 4-on-4 (two players per balance bench).

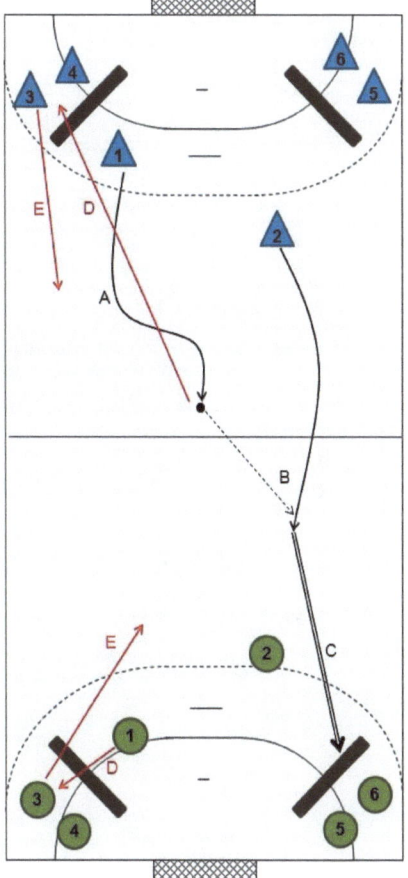

3. Sprint contests

No. 11	Sprint relay race with balance benches	6	★
	Topic: Sprint contests		
	Equipment required: 3 balance benches		

Course:

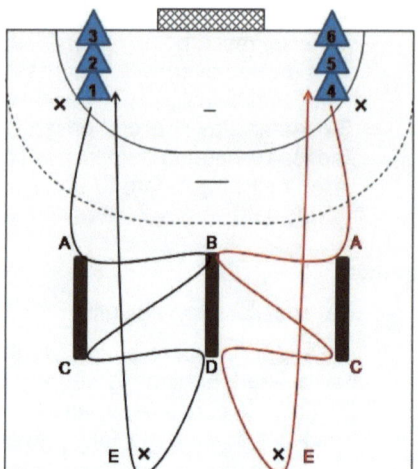

- On command, **1** and **4** start simultaneously and sprint straight forward towards the first corner of the balance bench (A).
- Then, they swiftly sidestep to the inner balance bench (corner) (B); afterwards, they sprint forward diagonally (corner) (C).
- Subsequently, they swiftly sidestep to the inner balance bench (corner) (D) before they eventually sprint around the cone, run back, and exchange a high-five with the next player (E).
- And so on.

⚠ The end of each balance bench should be touched lightly with one hand.

The losing team needs to do push-ups or sit-ups, for example.

No. 12	Going to Jerusalem	6	★
Topic:	Sprint contests		
Equipment required:	Foam beams (total number of players -1)		

Setting:
- Make three teams.
- Spread the foam beams across the court. There must be one foam beam less than there are players on the court (musical chairs principle).

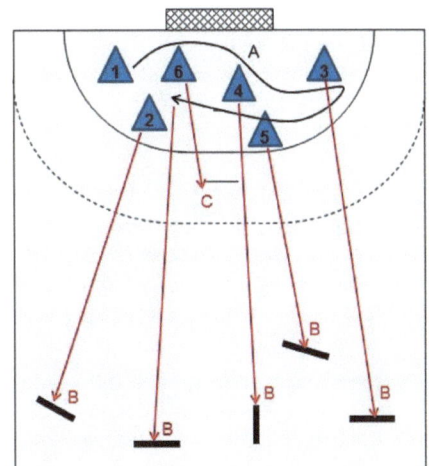

Course:
- The players crisscross throughout the goal zone at relaxed pace and "say hello" by exchanging high-fives (A).
- On command, the players start to run. They must try to be the first to stand on a certain foam beam and block it (B).
- The player who does not get a beam, drops out (C). Remove one beam then; the course needs to be repeated until only three players are left.
- The team that has the most players left on the field scores. If there is a tie (1 player left per team), each team scores.
- Spread the foam beams again and repeat the course three times.
- At the end, the team that scored highest wins the game. The two other teams need to perform a predetermined exercise (push-ups, jumping jacks, or similar).

⚠ If a player leaves the goal zone before the sign was given, he drops out immediately.

⚠ If two or more players step onto a foam beam almost at the same time, they need to come to an agreement about who was first; if they do not come to an agreement, they all drop out.

⚠ Team-internal running tactics could be helpful.

⚠ If there are many players, define exercises the drop-outs need to perform (strengthening exercises, endurance run, or similar).

From warm-up to handball team play
75 exercises for every handball training

No. 13	Team tag	10	★★
Topic:	Sprint contests		
Equipment required:			

Basic setting:
- Make 2 teams
- The center line is the "boundary" of the playing field.

Course:
- On command, one player per team (1 and 1) starts to run, crosses the center line (A), and tries to tag a player of the other team (B).
- If 1 succeeds (C), immediately runs back, and crosses the center line, the team has scored. Now, another player of the same team (3) is allowed to cross the center line in order to tag a player of the other team as fast as possible (D).

Tasks:
- Which team scores highest within 2 minutes?
- Each player of a team needs to tag 2 times (between the two "taggings", he needs to run back and cross the center line).

⚠ Only one player per team is allowed to cross the center line. If two players of the same team have crossed the center line, the team does not score, even one of them may have tagged an opponent!

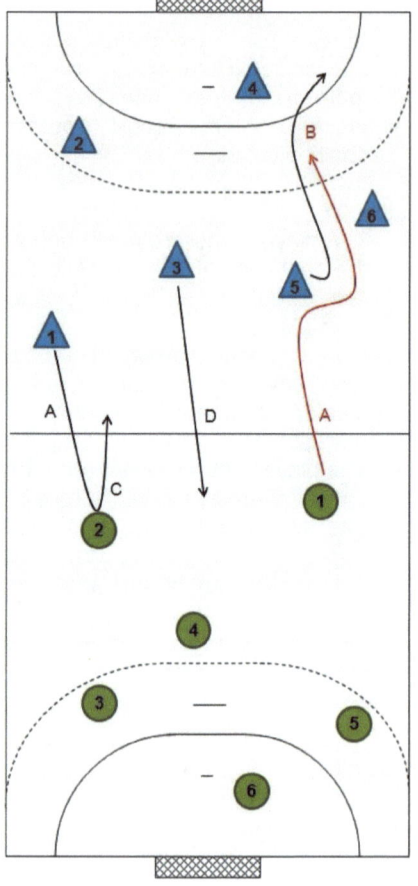

⚠ If 1 is in the "opponents'" half and is about to tag a player, he may not be tagged by 1. Players may only be tagged if they are in their own half of the playing field (and not in the opponents' half).

From warm-up to handball team play
75 exercises for every handball training

handball-uebungen.de

No. 14	Intensive sprint competition	6	★★★
Topic:	Sprint contests		
Equipment required:	5 to 8 small vaulting boxes, 1 handball per team of 2		

Setting:
- Make pairs; each pair has one handball.
- Position 5 to 8 small vaulting boxes upside down along the center line (see figure).

Course:
- On command, 1, 1, and 1 start to run from the goal zone simultaneously with their handball (A).
- 1, 1, and 1 sprint with their handball to the 1st box, put the ball inside (B), sprint back, and exchange high-fives with 2, 2, and 2, respectively (C), who have been waiting in the goal zone.

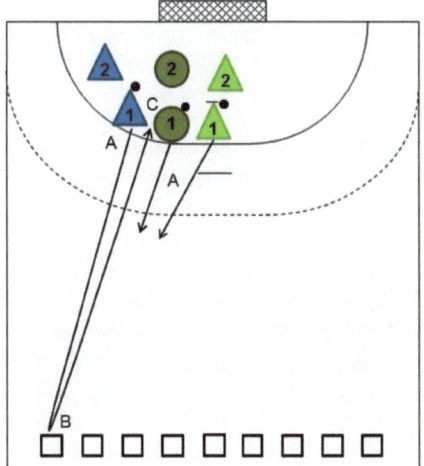

- Now 2, 2, and 2 (D) sprint to the 1st box, which contains the handballs. They **NEED** to fetch **THEIR** handball from the box (E), sprint back to the goal zone, and touch the 6-meter line with one foot (F). Only now they are allowed to hand over the handball to the first player.
- Subsequently, 1, 1, and 1 sprint to the 2nd box, put the ball inside (G), sprint back, exchange high-fives with 2, 2, and 2, respectively, who have been waiting in the goal zone (H).

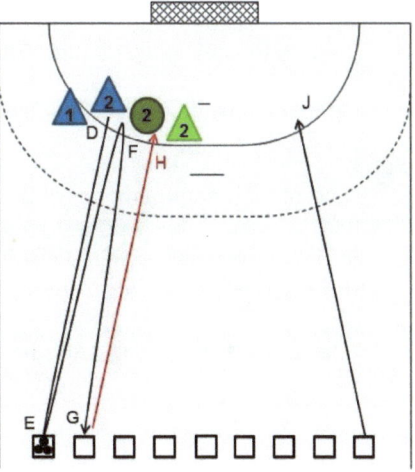

- And so on (until the last box is reached). The team that first brings their handball back from the last box to the goal zone (J) wins the game.

⚠ The exercise is quite exhausting.

⚠ If a ball drops out of the box, the player must put it back before he can continue. If the handball of another team drops out of the box during a move, the player needs to first put back this ball, too, before he can continue.

⚠ The players need to compete for space in a fair manner; this particularly applies to the first boxes (box 1 to 3), as there will be a lot of "traffic" around the boxes.

No. 15	Sprint competition with playing cards	6	★★
	Topic: Sprint contests		
	Equipment required: Timer, large vaulting box, deck of playing cards, 10 cones		

Preparation:
- Put the cards on top of the vaulting box with the reverse side of the cards facing upwards.
- Define the running paths for the suits of the flipped cards (diamonds, hearts, spades, clubs).

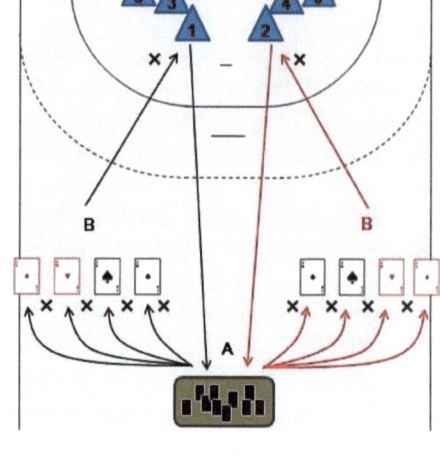

Course:
- On command, 1 and 2 start to run simultaneously and sprint to the vaulting box at the center line (A).
- Each player flips a card. Depending on the suit of the flipped card, the players need to sprint around the respective cone (e.g., clubs = sprint around the first cone, spades = sprint around the second cone) and back (B).
- Then it's the next player's turn. Each player has one (two) turn(s).

The losing team must do push-ups or sit-ups.

Variants:
- Hand out the same amount of playing cards to both teams in advance. They need to decide for themselves which player must run the short/long path (tactics). The player puts a card onto the vaulting box and, depending on the card's "value", runs around the respective cone and back, etc.

⚠ If a player runs the wrong path, he needs to go back and then run around the correct cone.

4. Coordination

No. 16	Sprint reaction with numbers	8	☆
	Topic: Coordination		
Equipment required:	10 cones		

Course 1 (figure 1):
- Once the coach has called out a number ("4" in the example), ▲1 and ▲2 simultaneously start to run at relaxed pace.
- ▲1 and ▲2 run to the 4th cone on their respective side and touch it (A). Then, both run to the center, exchange high-fives with both hands (B), and run back (C).

Course 2 (figure 2):
- This time, the players need to sprint. The first player who crosses the start line again wins the game. The loser must do an exercise (e.g., 3 push-ups).
- Once the coach has called out a number ("24" in the example), ▲1 and ▲2 simultaneously start to run again. The players need to run to the respective cones – hereby, the number of tens applies to the cones on the players' own side (D) and the number of ones to the cones on the opponents' side (E) –, touch them, and run back (F).

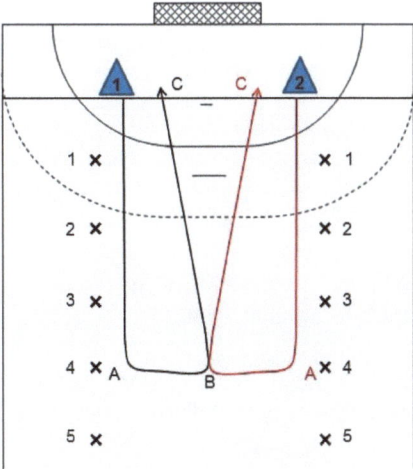

Figure 1

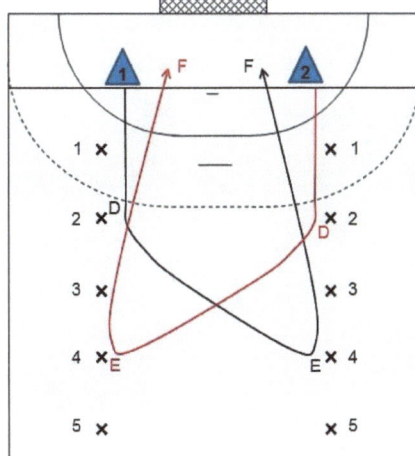

Figure 2

Course 3 (figure 3):
- Once the coach has called out a number ("325" in the example), 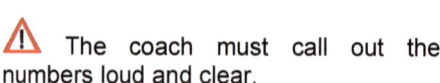 and simultaneously start to run again. The players need to run to the respective cones – hereby, the number of hundreds applies to the cones on the players' own side (G), the number of tens to the cones on the opponents' side (H), and the number of ones to the cones on the players' own side again (J) –, touch them, and run back (K).

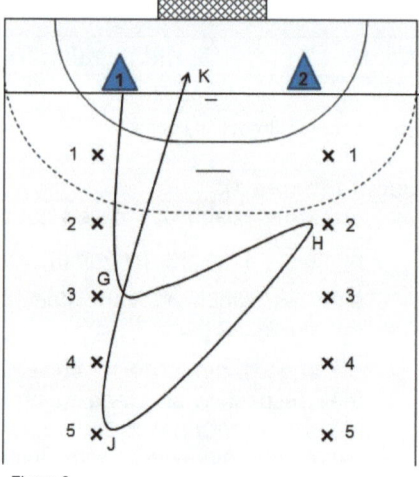

Figure 3

⚠ The coach must call out the numbers loud and clear.

⚠ During course 2 and 3, the players should meet in the center so that they need to fight their way to the next cone.

No. 17		Coordination reactions	8	★
	Topic:	Coordination		
	Equipment required:	3 small vaulting boxes, 4 cones, 1 whistle		

Course:

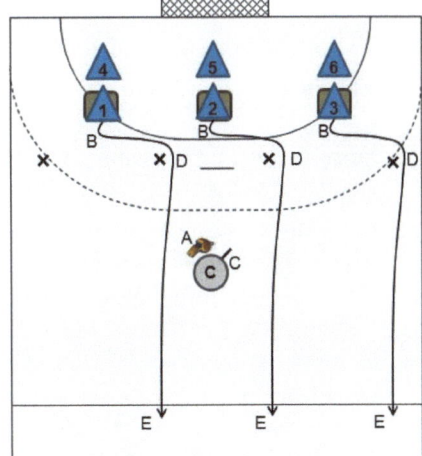

- 1, 2, and 3 each stand on a small vaulting box.
- Once C whistles (A), they jump down the box straight ahead at once (B).
- Immediately after he has whistled, and while the players are jumping, C raises one hand (right hand in the example (C)), which tells 1, 2, and 3 around which cone to run (D) before sprinting to the predefined finish line (E).
- The loser must do 10 quick jumping jacks (or push-ups, sit-ups, etc.) immediately after he has crossed the finish line. The players then run back at relaxed pace.
- Repeat the course with 4, 5, and 6, etc.

Variants:

- If C raises the right hand, the players need to run to the other side, i.e. they must run around the left cone rather than around the right cone.
- If C raises the right hand, the players need to run to the other side, i.e. they must run around the left cone rather than around the right cone. However, if C whistles a second time while raising his hand, the course changes again. The players then need to run around the right cone, as intended initially.

⚠ C must give the sign (raise the hand/whistle) early so that the players have enough time to react accordingly.

No. 18	Coordination run with defensive action	8	★
	Topic: Coordination		
	Equipment required: 1 coordination ladder, 9 hoops, 10 cones		

Course:

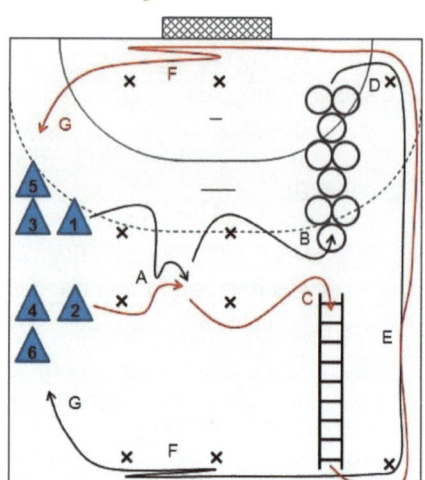

- 1 and 2 start simultaneously.
- 1 attacks 2 1-on-1, whereas 2 tries to push 1 aside and prevent him from breaking through the space between the cones (A).
- Afterwards, 1 and 2 run around their respective cone.
- 1 runs through the hoop course (one footstep per hoop) as fast as possible (B).
- 2 runs through the coordination ladder (two footsteps, i.e. left and right foot, per interspace) (C).
- Then, 1 and 2 run around the cone, start to sprint, and exchange high-fives (D and E).
- 1 and 2 run around the cone on the other side and towards the next cone at relaxed pace. As soon as they have arrived, they sprint to the 2nd cone (F), run back to the 1st cone backwards, and eventually sprint some meters before they line up again (G).
- 3 and 4 start delayed in order to not get in the other players' way.
- And so on.

No. 19		Coordination run	8	★★
	Topic:	Coordination		
Equipment required:		1 coordination ladder, 2 hurdles, 5 cones, 1 handball per player		

Course 1:

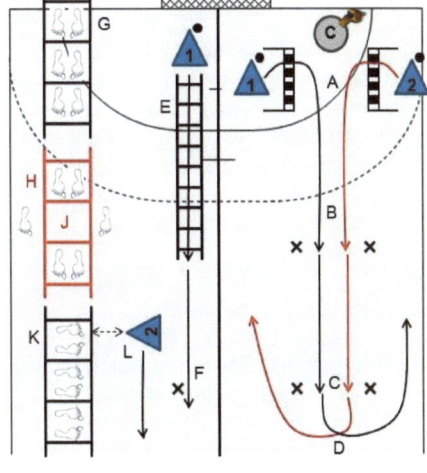

- 1 and 2 stand in front of the hurdle with both feet on the ground and the ball in their hands (face-to-face).
- Once the coach whistles, 1 and 2 start simultaneously, jump over the hurdle (A), and sidestep (facing each other) to the first cone while holding the ball above their heads (B).
- Once they arrive at the cone, both players turn around and sprint forward (dribbling) to the second cone. The loser immediately does five quick jumping jacks. Then both players join the line for the next course on the respective other side (D).
- Each player must do three courses on each side.

Afterwards, course 2 begins:

- 1 starts (dribbling) and runs through the coordination ladder (E); however, he must stick to the following rules:
  - Run through the coordination ladder as fast as possible, with two footsteps per interspace (left and right) (G), and move the handball around your hips in circles.
- Once 1 arrives at the end of the coordination ladder, he sprints (dribbling) to the cone (F) and then jogs back at slow pace.
- Each player must do two courses.

Further instructions for the next courses:

- Jump through the coordination ladder while doing jumping jacks (H). When your arms meet in the air during the jump movement (J), take the ball in your other hand, etc.
- Sidestep through the coordination ladder (two footsteps per interspace, (left and right) (K) while continuously passing and receiving the ball to/from a teammate (L).

No. 20	Ball coordination with five balls	2	★★★
Topic:	Coordination		
Equipment required:	5 handballs		

Course:
- Figure 1: The player on the right throws 2 handballs in the air and then throws a both-handed chest pass (arrow) with another handball to his counterpart. Shortly before he receives the chest pass, the left player throws both his handballs into the air (arrow).
- Figure 2: The left player catches the chest pass and immediately passes back to the right player (figure 3). Then he catches both his handballs from above.
- Now the right player throws both his handballs in the air, catches the chest pass (figure 4), and passes it back at once in order to catch his handballs from above.

⚠ Both players should stand still on both feet without moving them.

(Figure 1)

(Figure 2)

(Figure 3)

(Figure 4)

5. Ball familiarization

No. 21	Pass and run at signal	4	★
	Topic: Ball familiarization		
	Equipment required: 1 handball per team of 2		

Setting:
- The players stand pairwise, as shown in the figure, with each pair having one handball.

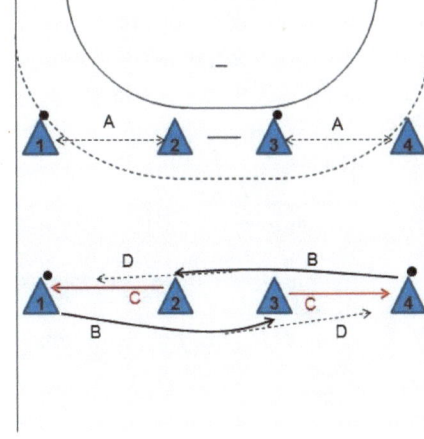

Course:
- 1 and 2 pass the ball while moving back and forth; so do 3 and 4 (A).
- On the coach's command, the players on the outer court (1 and 4) start to dynamically run forward and dribble to the other side (B).
- 2 and 3 take over the positions from 1 and 4 immediately (C).
- While moving forward, 1 and 4 pass the ball to 2 and 3 and take over their previous positions.
- Afterwards, 2 and 4 (1 and 3) pass the ball to each other in piston movement (A).

⚠ The players on the outer court should move forward more and more dynamically every time the coach gives a command.

No. 22	Pass and catch across the whole court in groups of 2	6	★
Topic:	Ball familiarization		
Equipment required:	1 handball per team of 2, 10 cones		

Course 1 (figure 1):
- ① and ② start together and run between their side line and their line of cones while passing and receiving the ball (A).
- At the end of the line of cones, ① and ② turn to one side (B and C), get closer together, and keep passing the ball (D). The players permanently need to change the passing variants (passing behind the back/over the head, between the legs, etc.).
- Afterwards, both players change sides and line up again (E).
- Each player must do 3 to 4 courses.

Variant:
- Jump shot pass (A)

Course 2 (figure 2):
- ① passes the ball into the path of ②, once he is immediately in front of the cone (F).
- ② makes an extensive running feint to one side of the cone while holding the ball (G) and then feints a stem shot.
- Afterwards, ② dribbles dynamically around the cone and passes the ball back to ① (H).
- Repeat the drill for the other cones.
- At the end of the line of cones, ① and ② turn to one side (B and C), get closer together, and keep passing the ball (D) (cf. course 1).
- Each player must do 3 to 4 courses.

Variant:
- Jump shot pass (H)

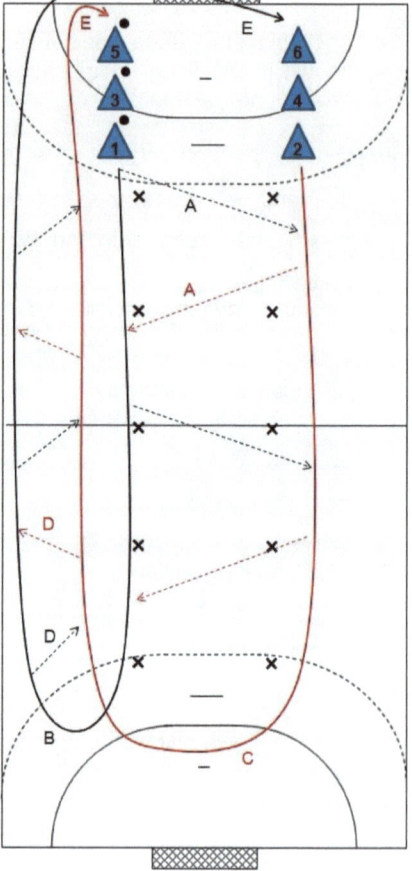

Figure 1

Course 3 (figure 3):

- 1 and 2 start together and do a slalom run through the line of cones while passing the ball (J and K).
- The distance between 1 and 2 should always remain the same. 2 needs to run far afield and keep the distance to 1.

⚠ After the first cone, 1 must considerably speed up and run far afield (M) in order to keep the distance while 2 is running around the cone (L).

- Repeat the drill for the other cones.
- At the end of the line of cones, 1 and 2 turn to one side (B and C), get closer together, and keep passing the ball (D) (cf. course 1).
- Each player must do 3 to 4 courses.

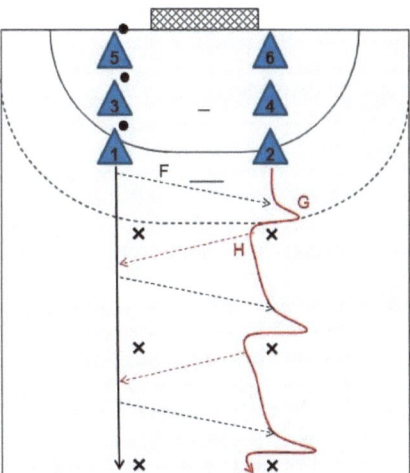
Figure 2

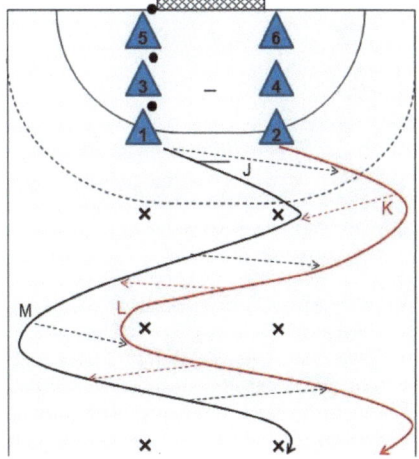
Figure 3

No. 23 — Dynamic group piston movement — 8 ★★

Topic:	Ball familiarization
Equipment required:	1 handball per player, 4 cones

Course 1:

- 1 makes a dynamic piston movement forward (A) and passes the ball into the piston movement path of 3 (B).
- After the pass (A), 1 immediately moves back and lines up behind 5 again (C).
- 3 also makes a dynamic piston movement forward and passes the ball to 5 (D), etc.
- 4 starts simultaneously with 1 and makes the same movements (E).

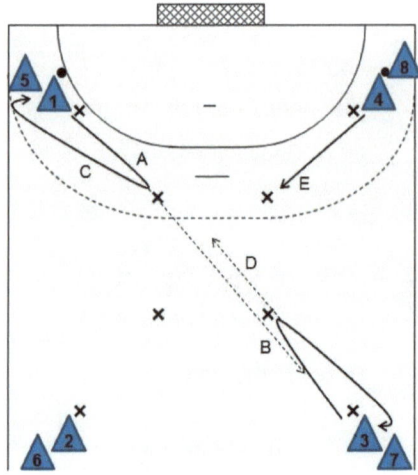

Course 2:

- 2 runs forward dynamically while 1 passes the ball into his running path (F).
- 2 makes a running feint to the left side of the cone while holding the ball (he must not bounce it), feints a stem shot (G), dribbles dynamically around the cone, makes a piston movement forward (H), and eventually passes the ball into the piston movement path of 3 (J).
- 3 repeats the movements and passes to 4 (K).
- And so on.

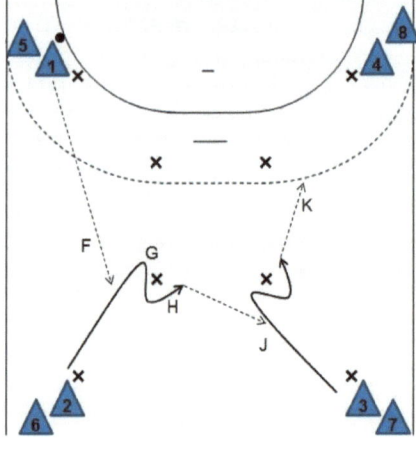

⚠ The piston movement (A and B) to the cone must be carried out dynamically; the pass (B and D) should be initiated with a stem shot feint.

No. 24	Running feint with subsequent catch and pass in full speed	8	★★
	Topic: Ball familiarization		
	Equipment required: 1 handball (2 handballs), 8 cones		

Course:

- 2 starts without a ball, makes a dynamic running feint to the left (A), then runs in the opposite direction, and receives a pass from 3 into his running path (B).
- 2 passes the ball to 4 and lines up again (C).
- After he played the pass to 2 (B), 3 starts at once, makes a dynamic running feint to the left (D), then runs in the opposite direction, and receives the pass from 4 into his running path (E).
- 3 passes the ball to 1 and lines up behind (F).
- After he played the pass (E), 4 starts the same drill, etc.

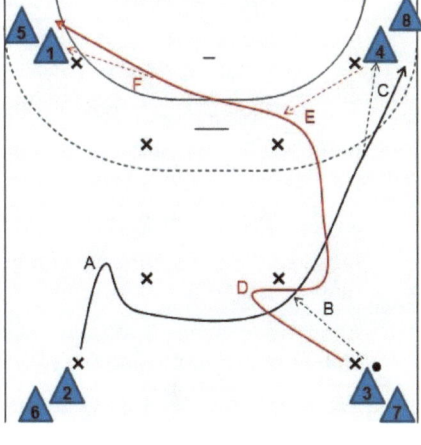

Variant:

- Start the course with two handballs at a time. 1 and 3 each have a handball; 2 and 4 start with the running feint, etc.
- The players run to the left.

⚠ Keep increasing the speed during the exercise.

No. 25	Pass and catch across the whole court with goalkeeper	9	★★
Topic:	Ball familiarization		
Equipment required:	1 handball per player, 2 cones		

Course:

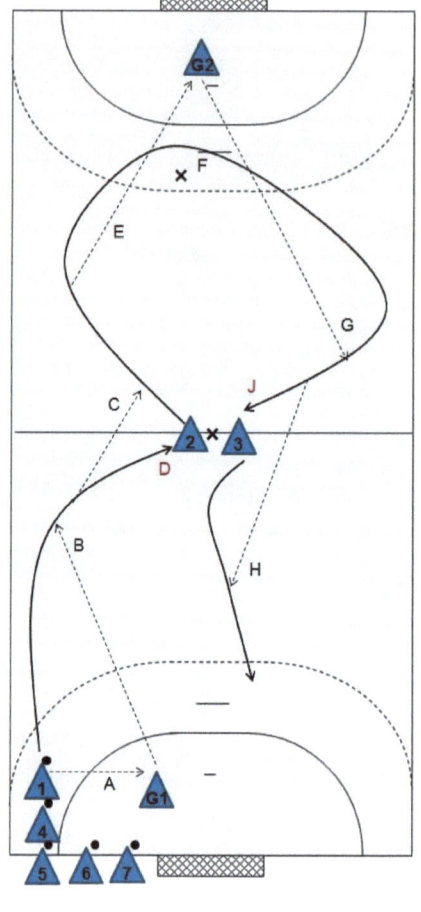

- 1 plays a pass to the goalkeeper G1 (A) and starts to run forward dynamically.
- The goalkeeper G1 passes the ball back to 1, into his running path (B).
- 2 starts dynamically and receives the pass from 1 into his running path (C).
- After he played the pass, 1 stands at the center line (D).
- While running, 2 throws a pass to the other goalkeeper G2 (E) and runs around the cone (F). The goalkeeper G2 passes the ball back into his running path (G).
- 3 starts and receives a pass from 2 into his running path (H).
- After he played the pass, 2 stands at the center line (J).
- After he finished the course, 3 lines up again.
- 4 starts the same course (delayed). The players should only have to wait at the center line for a little while before they receive the next pass (C and G); the start must be coordinated accordingly.

⚠ The players should run at full speed and pass the ball they received as fast as possible.

6. Goalkeeper warm-up shooting

No. 26	Running exercise with subsequent shot	8	★
	Topic: Goalkeeper warm-up shooting		
Equipment required:	3 cones, 1 handball per player		

Course:

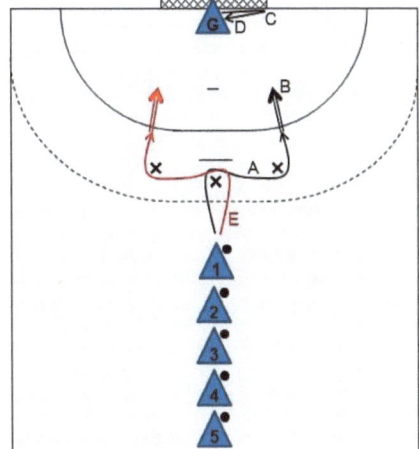

- 1 starts to dribble the ball and dynamically runs around both cones (A).
- After the second cone, 1 runs to the 6-meter line at high pace and shoots at the right side of the goal as instructed (top, middle, bottom) (B).
- The goalkeeper G stands in the center of the goal, tries to react accordingly and to save 1's ball (B and C). The goalkeeper G then goes back to the center of the goal (D).
- As soon as 1 has run around the first cone, 2 starts the same drill and shoots at the left side of the goal as instructed (E).
- Repeat until each player has shot one time.

⚠️ The goalkeeper G should be able to react from the center of the goal. Therefore, the attacking players must coordinate their running and shooting in order to provide him with a series of shots.

No. 27	Two-position warm-up shooting	8	★★
Topic:	Goalkeeper warm-up shooting		
Equipment required:	1 handball per player, foam beams (to indicate the wing position)		

Course:

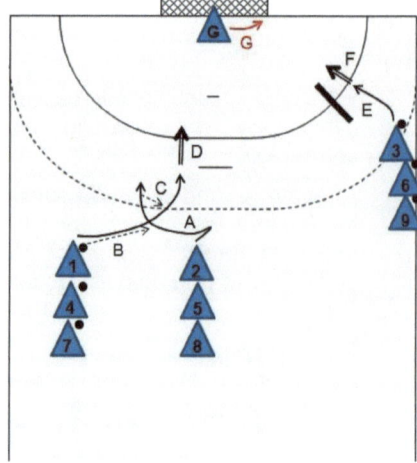

- 2 initiates a crossing (A) and receives a pass from 1 into his running path (B).
- 1 takes on the crossing, receives a pass from 2 (C), and shoots at the left side of the goal as instructed (top, bottom, free choice) (D).
- Immediately after the shot, 3 starts to run to the 6-meter line (E) and shoots from the wing position (F).
- After 1 has shot, the goalkeeper immediately jumps to the short corner of the goal and tries to save the ball (G).
- Start over the course, again beginning with the crossing.
- 1 lines up on the wing position, 3 lines up behind 8, and 2 lines up behind 7.
- Repeat the course several times, then change the starting point to the right side of the court.

⚠ The players on the wing position need to time their shot, i.e. the goalkeeper must be able to save the ball, however, he must also move quickly to the short corner of the goal after the shot from the LB/RB positions.

No. 28	Dynamic warm-up shooting with subsequent fast break initiation	8	★★
	Topic: Goalkeeper warm-up shooting		
Equipment required:	1 handball per player		

Setting:
- The players line up between the 6- and 9-meter line, each holding a handball.

Course:
- ▲1 starts from the wing position. At the beginning, the goalkeeper ▲G1 stands slightly closer to the center of the goal.
- ▲1 shoots the ball top left (A); the goalkeeper ▲G1 makes a small step to the right and tries to save the ball (B).
- ▲2 then shoots top right (delayed) (C). The players must not shoot into the goal corners; the goalkeeper ▲G1 must be able to save the shot top right with only a small step (D).
- ▲3 then shoots top left again (delayed) (E). At the end of the series of 4 shots, ▲4 shoots top right (F).
- After he has shot, ▲4 runs a fast break at once (G).
- After the 4th shot, the goalkeeper ▲G1 immediately fetches a ball, goes into a good throwing position (H) (diagonal pass), and then passes the ball into ▲4's running path (J).
- ▲4 shoots at the goal (K).
- Afterwards, the next group of 4 (▲5, ▲6, ▲7, and ▲8) starts the same course on the right side.

⚠ During the series of 4 shots, the players need to make sure that the goalkeeper ▲G1 can move from shot to shot in the most optimal way. The goalkeeper ▲G1 should be able to save the balls using a proper technique.

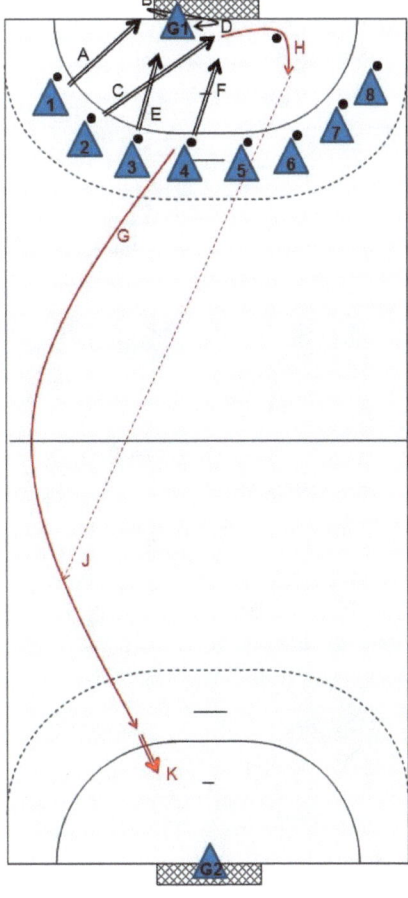

No. 29	Warm-up shooting with defense exercise	8	★★
	Topic: Goalkeeper warm-up shooting		
Equipment required:	3 cones, 1 ball per player		

Course:

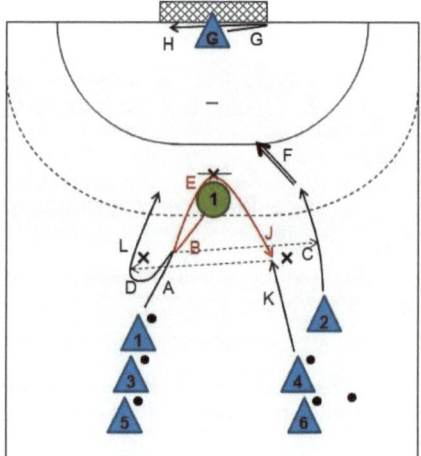

- 1 starts a dynamic piston movement (A).
- 1 steps forward into the piston movement of 1 and attacks 1 (B).
- 1 passes the ball into the running path of 2 (C).
- After he has played the pass, 1 moves back immediately (D).
- 2 dynamically approaches the goal and shoots at the left side of the goal as instructed (top, middle, or bottom) (F).
- While 1 plays the pass (C), the goalkeeper G first moves dynamically to the goalpost (G) and then moves to the right in order to save 2's ball (H). Afterwards, the goalkeeper G goes back to the center of the goal and repeats the movement (in the opposite direction) as 1 shoots from the other side.
- After the 1st action (B), 1 immediately moves backwards to the cone (E), steps forward into the piston movement (K) of 4, and attacks 4 (J).
- 4 passes the ball into the running path of 1 (L), who then also shoots at the goal (right side).
- Repeat until each player has shot. Then change the defensive player. Repeat until each player has played defense one time.

Shooting variants for the attacking players:

- Shoot at the short goalpost/corner (the goalkeeper's G running path then changes).
- Shoot uninterruptedly from the 9-meter line. After receiving the pass (C), the attacking players should make one step only and then throw a jump shot from the 9-meter line (F).

⚠ Make sure that 1 moves correctly in the defense (move foot and arm towards the throwing hand).

⚠ 1 should tackle the attacking players in a highly dynamic manner and clearly interrupt their movements (simultaneous training for the attacking players who are to play a proper pass while being tackled).

From warm-up to handball team play
75 exercises for every handball training

No. 30	"Intelligent" warm-up shooting (on instruction) with subsequent fast break	8	★★
	Topic:	Goalkeeper warm-up shooting	
Equipment required:	1 handball per player		

Setting:

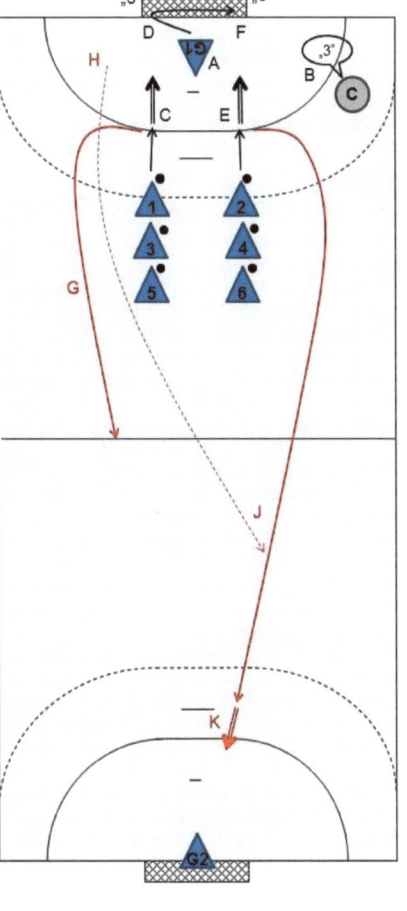

- The goalkeeper G1 stands with his back turned at the players.
- The players need to shoot a series of 4 shots sticking to the following rules: If C calls out an uneven number:
    o 1st player shoots top left.
    o 2nd player shoots top right.
    o 3rd player shoots bottom left.
    o 4th player shoots bottom right.
- If C calls out an even number, the course is to be done the other way round:
    o 1st player shoots top right.
    o 2nd player shoots top left, etc.
- The players need to pay attention to the number the coach calls out and start accordingly:
- Uneven number: 1 starts.
- Even number: 2 starts.

Course:

- The goalkeeper G1 does fast jumping jacks (A) on the spot.
- C calls out a number ("3" in the example). This is the sign for the goalkeeper G1 to turn around at once and to get in position in the goal as well as for 1 to start the series of shots top left (C).
- The goalkeeper G1 tries to save the 1st ball (top left) (D).
- 2 shoots top right (delayed) (E).
- The goalkeeper G1 moves to the side (sidesteps) and tries to save the ball (F).
- 3 shoots bottom left (delayed).

- At the end, 4 shoots bottom right.
- After they have shot, 1, 2, and 3 sprint to the center line at once (G).
- After he has shot, 4 runs a fast break at once, receives a long pass from G1 (J), and shoots at the goal (K).
- Afterwards, it's the next four players' turn.

⚠ The goalkeeper G1 should be in a good throwing position before throwing the long pass. His position should allow him to play a diagonal pass (H), since, for 4, a diagonal pass is easier to catch.

Variant:
- Set calculation tasks for the shooting, e.g., "5 plus 8".

7. Offense/series of shots

No. 31	Simple series of shots with coordination run	8	★
	Topic: Offense/series of shots		
	Equipment required: 6 cones, ball box with sufficient number of handballs		

Setting:
- Use two cones to define each running path (it should form an "8").
- Put two more cones on the floor to define the running path for the subsequent action (see figure).

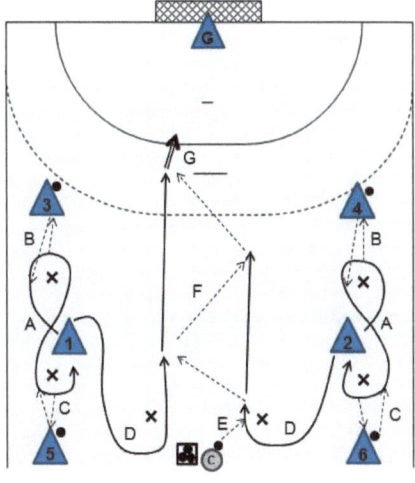

Course:
- 1 and 2 start simultaneously; their running path around the two cones should form an "8" (A).
- While running, they alternately play double passes (B and C) with the receivers (3 and 5, 4 and 6, respectively).
- Once the coach whistles, 1 and 2 run around the cones in the back without a ball (D).
- The coach passes a ball to one of the players (E). 1 and 2 keep running towards the goal and pass to each other (F) until one of them is in shooting position (G).
- As soon as the coach has whistled, one receiver each starts running the "8 path". A new player becomes the second receiver and the course starts over.

⚠ The players should run the "8 path" smoothly (A). Also, they should not interrupt their running moves when they play and receive a pass.

⚠ On command, the players should run around the cones and pass the ball as fast as they can (D) until one of them shoots at the goal (E, F, and G).

No. 32	Series of shots on instruction	8	★
	Topic: Offense/series of shots		
Equipment required:	4 cones, ball box with sufficient number of handballs, 1 small vaulting box		

Basic course:
- Three players do the course in a row; afterwards, change the players.
- The remaining players (6 and 7, etc.) fetch the balls and provide the receiver (4) with balls (via 5).
- Assign numbers to the goal corners (1 to 4).
- Put a small vaulting box into one bottom corner of the opposite goal; it serves as a shooting target.

Course:
- 1 starts without a ball, runs around the cone (A), and receives a pass from 4 into his running path (C).
- While 1 runs around the cone, C – who is standing next to the goal – calls out a number ("1" in the example) (B).
- This is the sign for the goalkeeper G to start. G dynamically sidesteps from the center of the goal to the goalpost opposite to the number called out, touches it lightly (D), and then immediately sidesteps back to the other side (F). Now, he tries to save the ball that is shot by 1 according to C 's instruction ("1" = top left, from the attacking player's view) (E).
- After 1 has shot (E), he immediately runs around the next cone (G) and receives a pass from 4 into his path (H).
- While 1 runs around the cone (G), C calls out the next number, i.e. shooting instruction.
- 1 shoots as instructed (J) and the goalkeeper G moves to the opposite goalpost as done before.

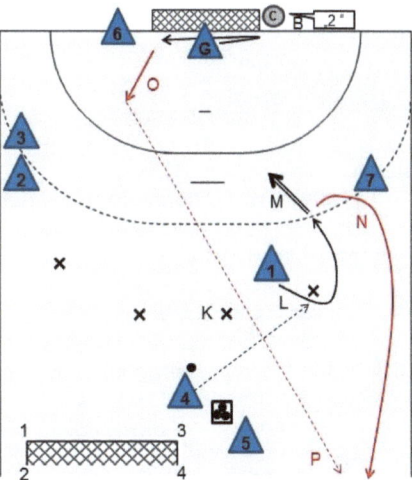

- 1 repeats the course for the 3rd (K) and 4th cone (L and M).
- After his 4th shot, 1 runs a fast break immediately (N).
- The goalkeeper G fetches one of the unused balls (O) and passes it into 1's path (P). 1 approaches the opposite goal and shoots at the small vaulting box.

⚠ The goalkeeper's G basic position is the center of the goal; i.e. he always must get back there before the next shot.

⚠ C must call out the numbers in such a way that the goalkeeper G can run to the goalpost and save the ball.

No. 33	Series of shots with extended coordination run	8	★★
	Topic:	Offense/series of shots	
Equipment required:	2 coordination ladders, 2 cones, ball box with sufficient number of handballs		

Setting:
- Put the two coordination ladders on the floor and align them in parallel. Position two cones, one on the left and one on the right, as shown in the figure.
- The coach stands at the side next to the ball box that contains additional handballs.

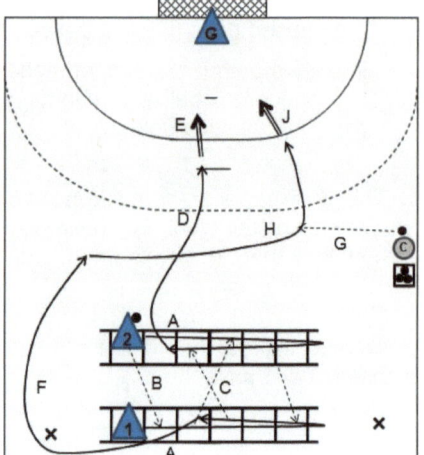

Course:
- **1** and **2** sidestep (face-to-face) through the coordination ladder (two footsteps per interspace) (A) while passing the ball (B, C).
- At the end of the coordination ladder, the players change the direction and sidestep to the other side.
- On the coach's command ("GO"), the player who has the ball (here **2**) runs towards the goal (D) and shoots (E).
- The other player (**1**) runs around one of the two cones (F).
- The coach rolls another ball into the court (G), **1** picks it up (H), runs towards the goal, and shoots (J).
- On the coach's command "GO" for **1** and **2**, the next two players immediately start to pass and sidestep through the coordination ladder.

⚠️ The players should react immediately on the coach's command and start the respective subsequent action.

From warm-up to handball team play
75 exercises for every handball training

No. 34	Complex all-position series of shots	8	★★★
	Topic: Offense/series of shots		
	Equipment required: 4 cones, ball box with sufficient number of handballs		

Basic course:
- The individual shots should be thrown in short intervals.
- One defensive player per middle sector (preferably a back player and a pivot who switch regularly)
- All players must shoot from their respective position in the following order: LW, pivot left, LB, pivot right, RB, RW.
- Each pivot should shoot from both sides.

Course on the wing positions (figure 1):

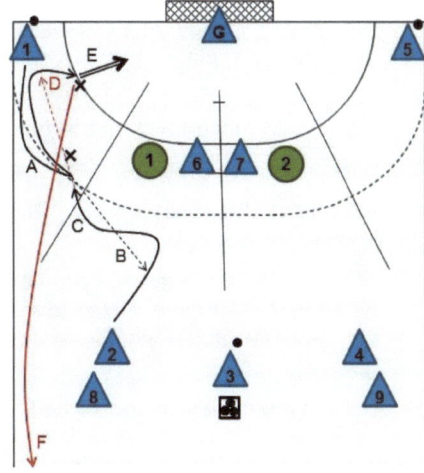

Figure 1

- ▲1 makes a curved piston movement (A) and passes the ball to ▲2 who makes a piston movement towards the center (B).
- ▲2 feints a shooting and then dynamically dribbles towards the wing position (C).
  ⚠ ▲2 must receive the pass in such a way that he does not have to dribble before feinting the shot.
- ▲2 passes the ball into the running path of ▲1 (D) who has immediately moved back to the wing position after playing the initial pass.
- ▲1 shoots at the goal (E), immediately runs a fast break, receives a pass from the goalkeeper ⚫G into his running path, and eventually shoots at the opposite goal (F).
- Afterwards, the next player starts the same course on the LW position.

Course on the left back position for the pivot (figure 2):

- 2 receives a pass from 3 into his running path (H).
- 1 should clearly move towards the attacking player's movement (G).
- 2 should move towards the goal until he almost reaches 1 and then pass the ball around 1's body to the pivot (J).
- 6 leaves his starting position near the 7-meter line, picks up the ball, and eventually shoots at the goal (K).
- Repeat the course on the same side with 7.

Figure 2

Course on the left back position for the back position players (figure 3):

- 2 makes a dynamic piston movement towards the left (M) and receives a pass into his running path (L).
- 1 should clearly move towards 2's movement (N).
- 2 makes an extensive shooting feint (M).
- 6 leaves his starting position at the 7-meter line, moves forward along with 1, and places a screen on the inner side (O).

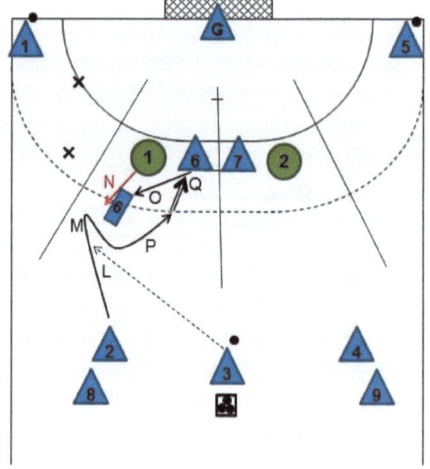

Figure 3

- 2 dynamically runs (dribbles) to the inner side around the screening of 6, then approaches the goal (P), and eventually makes a jump shot from the 9-meter line (Q).
- Afterwards, it's the turn of the next back position player. Each player must do the course twice (two shots).
- Repeat the course on the right side.

⚠ Change the players on the back positions as well as the receivers regularly.

⚠ The individual courses should be performed quickly and without a break; the other players should not have to wait for too long.

From warm-up to handball team play
75 exercises for every handball training

No. 35	**Intensive series of shots after previous exertion**	8	★★★
	Topic:	Offense/series of shots	
	Equipment required:	6 hurdles (alternatively: small vaulting boxes), 1 handball per player	

Setting:
- Position the hurdles (or small vaulting boxes) as shown in the figure.
- Divide the team into three groups:
  o Two shooting exercise groups (1, 2, 3, and 4, 5, 6)
  o One strengthening exercise group (7, 8, and 9)

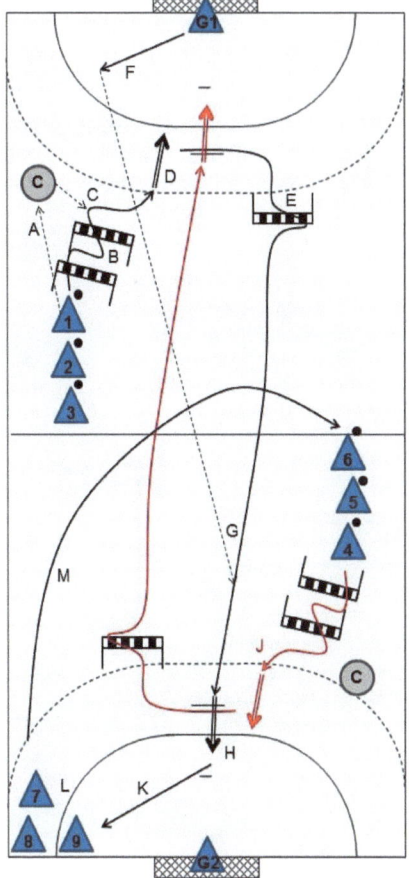

Course:
- 1 passes his handball to C (A) and jumps over both hurdles (with both legs at the same time) without making an intermediate hop between the hurdles (the players may touch the floor between the hurdles one time only) (B).
- 4 starts the same course in parallel with 1 (J).
- While jumping over the second hurdle, 1 receives a return pass from C, shortly before he touches the ground again (C). 1 must land with both feet.
- Now, 1 starts to run towards the goal, without dribbling however (i.e. observing the 3-step rule), and eventually makes a jump shot (D).
- After the shot, 1 jumps over the hurdle with both legs (E), dynamically starts to run a fast break, receives a long pass from the goalkeeper G1 (G), and eventually shoots at the opposite goal (H).
- The goalkeeper's G1 position should allow him to play the long pass in an optimal way (i.e. diagonally) (F).

- After he has shot, ▲1 joins the strengthening exercise group on the side (K) and does 10 push-ups and 10 sit-ups alternately. ▲7 gets up and joins the 1st shooting exercise group (M).
- After he has shot, ▲4 lines up again behind ▲3.
- Repeat until each player has been in each group 10 to 15 times.

⚠ Adjust hurdle height to the players' level of performance; i.e. in such a way that the players can jump over the hurdles with both legs at the same time.

⚠ Both shooting exercise groups must start simultaneously in order to give the goalkeepers enough time to position themselves correctly after they have thrown the long pass for the fast break.

⚠ During the exercise, all players must be highly concentrated in order to prevent collisions on the running paths.

8. General offense

No. 36	Back and forth (piston) movement with subsequent wing player shot	8	★
	Topic: General offense		
	Equipment required: 2 cones, ball box with sufficient number of handballs		

Course:

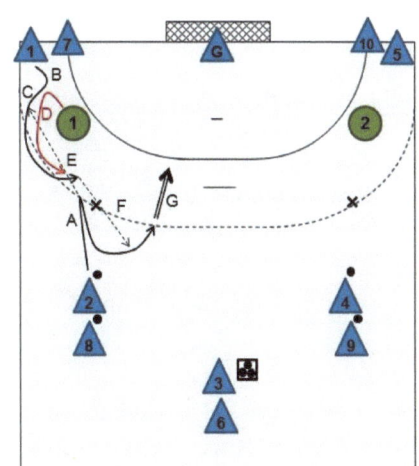

- ▲2 makes a piston movement with the ball towards the left side of the cone (A) and passes the ball into ▲1's running path (C).
- On the wing position, ▲1 should first run towards the goal before he receives the pass (B).
- After he has received the ball, ▲1 runs around ●1. Then he makes a dynamic piston movement between ●1 and the cone (E).
- ●1 runs along with ▲1 and interrupts the piston movement (D).
- Following his initial pass (C), ▲2 immediately moves back again, makes a counter movement towards the center, where he receives the ball from ▲1 (F), and eventually makes a jump shot at the goal (G).

Subsequent action for the wing player:

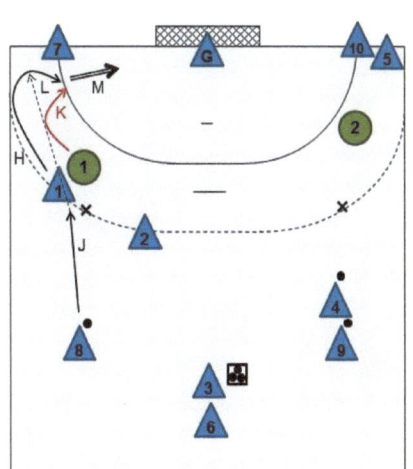

- Following his pass (F), ▲1 immediately moves back to the wing position (H).
- ▲8 makes a piston movement with the ball towards the left side of the cone (J) and passes the ball into ▲1's running path (L).
- ▲1 shoots at the goal from the wing position (M).
- ●1 also immediately moves back to the wing position (K), allows ▲1 to shoot, but tries to slightly interfere with the shot.
- Repeat the course on the other side.
- As soon as it is turn of the left side players again, repeat the course with ▲8 and ▲7.
- Afterwards, ▲1 and ▲7 as well as ▲2 and ▲8 switch positions, etc.

Variants:

- 1️⃣ may break through on the right (outer) side, if 1️⃣ gives way (N).
- If 1️⃣ does not strictly follow 1️⃣'s movements to the inner side, 1️⃣ may break through on the inner side (O).
- Decision-making exercise for 1️⃣ (break through on the outer side, break through on the inner side, or passing the ball to 2️⃣, if breaking through is not possible at all).

⚠️ During the exercise, 1️⃣ and 2️⃣ should play more and more offensively against 1️⃣ and 5️⃣.

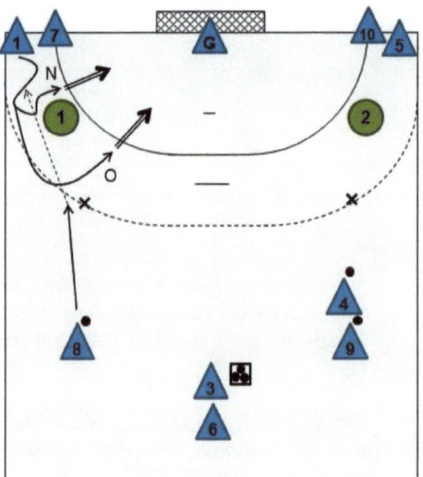

No. 37	2-on-2 team play with additional exercises	6	★
	Topic: General offense		
	Equipment required: 1 coordination ladder, 2 foam beams, sufficient number of handballs		

Setting:
- Position a coordination ladder on the center line. Put foam beams to the left and right.
- Make two teams and name them (here "blue" team and "green" team).

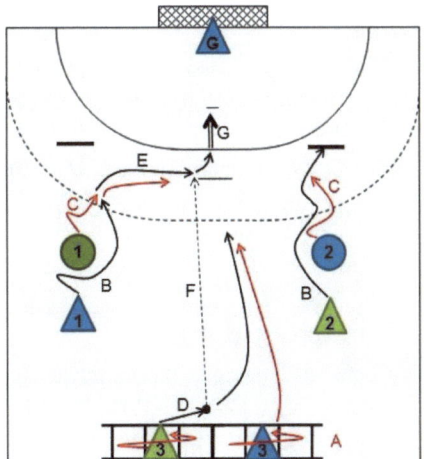

Course:
- On the coach's command ("GO"), three actions start simultaneously.
- 3 and 3 jump through the coordination ladder: to the left, back to the middle, to the right, back to the middle, and so on (A).
- Both players stand with their backs turned to the other players so that they cannot see their actions.
- 1 tries to break through 1's defense 1-on-1 without a ball (B) and tries to touch the foam beam with one foot. 1 tries to defend the beam as long as possible (C).
- 2 tries the same, attacking the defensive player of the blue team however.
- Once a player touches a beam, he calls out his team's name (in the figure, 2 manages to touch the beam, he calls out "green").
- This is the sign for 3 to pick up the ball (D) and to, together with 1, play 2-on-2 against 1 and 3 and try to score a goal (E, F, and G).
- If they manage to shoot a goal, the green team scores.
- Afterwards, each team substitutes one player for each of the three positions, additional players join the game, and the course starts over on the coach's command ("GO").
- Which team scores highest?

⚠ The players who have not been involved in the successful 1-on-1 action play 2-on-2 (2 has touched the beam, 1 and 3 play 2-on-2 against 1 and 3). The successful attacking player and his defensive counterpart do not participate in the 2-on-2 play towards the goal.

⚠ After the successful attack on the foam beam, the players must adjust immediately and play 2-on-2.

No. 38	Simple crossing with decision-making: RB/LB and wing player	8	★★
Topic:	General offense		
Equipment required:	2 cones, ball box with sufficient number of handballs		

Course:

- ③ passes the ball into ②'s running path to the center (A) (the cone serves for orientation) (B).
- ② dynamically moves with the ball towards the wing position. ① runs a curve from the wing position (C), takes on the crossing of ②, and receives a pass into his running path (D).
- ① dynamically approaches the goal with the ball and makes a jump shot (E). ① serves as defensive block.
- Afterwards, repeat the course on the other side with ③, ④, and ⑤.
- ① and ② subsequently switch positions.
- And so on.

Fixed extension:

- After the crossing, ① passes the ball into ③'s path forward (F).
- ③ makes a jump shot at the goal (G). ② serves as defensive block.

Optional extension:

- With his action, ① determines the further movements of ①:
  - If ① remains defensive, ① makes a jump shot at the goal (E).
  - If ① actively steps forward, he passes the ball to ③ (F) who then makes a jump shot at the goal (G).

⚠ ① must offensively approach the goal before he passes to ③ (F).

No. 39	Simple crossing with continued playing: CB and wing player	11	★★
	Topic:	General offense	
	Equipment required:	2 ball boxes with sufficient number of handballs	

Course:

- ▲4 makes a piston movement with the ball to the left and passes the ball into the running path of ▲3 (A) who makes a dynamic piston movement towards the far left.
- After passing the ball, ▲4 immediately moves back to his initial position (D).
- ▲1 dynamically runs a curve from the wing position, takes on the crossing from ▲3, and receives a pass (B).
- ▲2 runs a wide curve to the center and dynamically approaches the goal while receiving the pass from ▲1 into his path (C).
- ▲4 makes a parallel piston movement and receives the ball from ▲2 into his path (E).
    - If ●2 remains defensive at the 6-meter line, ▲4 shoots at the goal at full speed (F).
    - If ●2 moves towards ▲4 offensively (G), ▲4 bounces the ball to ▲5 on the wing position (H) who runs a curve and eventually shoots at the goal (J).
- Repeat the course on the other side.
- And so on.

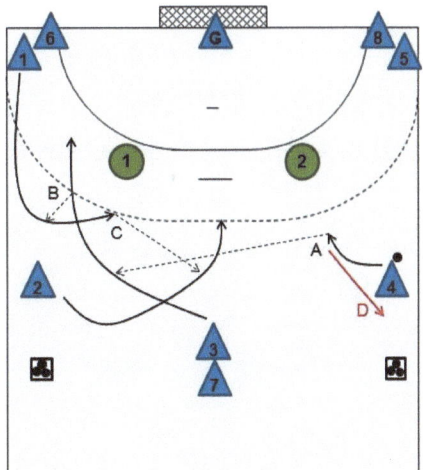

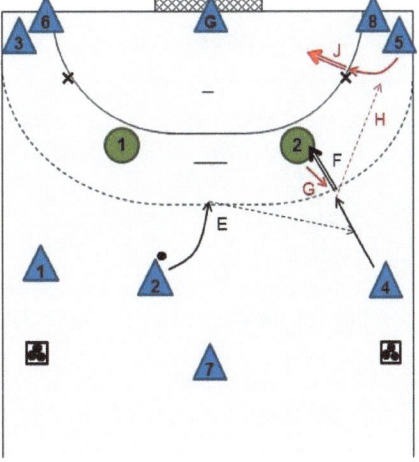

⚠ ●1 and ●2 should keep varying their movements and force the attacking players to react accordingly (shoot at the goal or pass to the wing position).

No. 40	Russian screen in the HL/HR positions – Initiation	8	★★
	Topic: General offense		
	Equipment required: 8 cones, ball box with sufficient number of handballs		

Course:

- ① dynamically runs towards the cone and receives a pass from ⑤ into his path (A).
- As soon as he is in line with the cone, ① feints a stem shot (plants left foot firmly on the ground and feints a shot) (B).
- ① should move towards ①'s piston movement (C).
- ① dribbles around ① dynamically; ① must force his defensive counterpart to move along with him (D)!
- ⑥ steps forward and screens off ① so that he cannot move any further (C and E).
- ⑥ leaves his screening position next to ①, moves back towards the 6-meter line (F), and receives a pass from ① directed at the goal zone (G).
- ⑥ shoots at the goal (H).
- Afterwards, repeat the drill on the other side (J).

⚠ ① must not dribble the ball before he feints the stem shot (B)!

⚠ ⑥ may screen off ① with his body only (E), he must not use his arms (offensive foul).

⚠ ⑥ should not receive a direct pass, but rather a bouncing pass towards the 6-meter line (G) so that ⑥ can pick up the ball while moving and can shoot immediately.

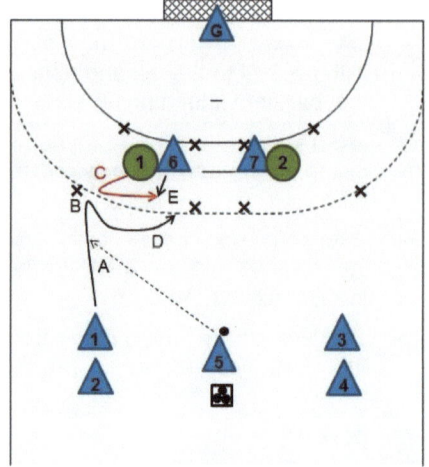

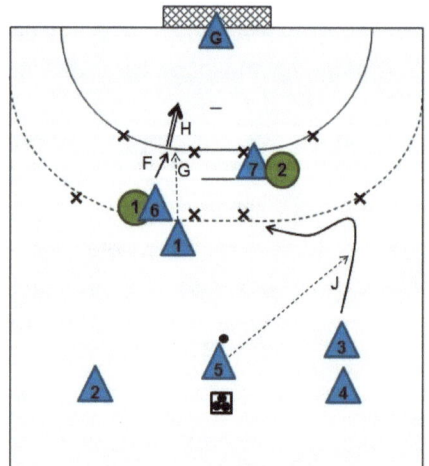

No. 41	Russian screen in the HL/HR positions – Subsequent action	8	★★
Topic:	General offense		
Equipment required:	6 cones, ball box with sufficient number of handballs		

Course:

- 6 stands in normal position and screens off 2.
- 1 starts a dynamic move and receives a pass from 5 into his running path (A).
- On the left side, next to 1, 1 feints a stem shot at the goal (B).
- 1 should clearly move towards 1 (C).
- 1 dribbles around 1 and dynamically approaches the goal (D).
- 6 leaves his position next to 2 and places a screen on the inner side of 1's running path (E).
    - If 2 remains defensive at the 6-meter line, 1 makes a jump shot at the goal (F).
    - If 2 actively steps forward (H) to block 1's shot (F), 1 plays a bouncing pass around 2 towards the goal zone (J). 6 leaves his screening position next to 1 (E), moves back towards the 6-meter line and towards the ball (K), picks up the ball, and shoots at the goal (L).
- Repeat the drill on the other side with 2 changing the side (G) – now making up the defense together with 3.

⚠ If 1 does not offensively move towards 1's path (C), 1 may also break through on the left side of 1 or make a jump shot from the 9-meter line.

⚠ 6 must not use his hands in order to screen off his counterpart sideways (E) (offensive foul). Preferably, he should cross his arms over his chest.

No. 42	3-on-3 simple crossing	7	★★
Topic:	General offense		
Equipment required:	6 cones, ball box with sufficient number of handballs		

Basic course:

- ①, ② and ③ play 3-on-3 against ①, ② and ③.
- The crossing and running paths below should always be the initial action. Afterwards, the players should play freely and creatively.
- In the beginning, the distance between the cones may be longer in order to make the course easier for the attacking players. Decrease the size of the playing field over time.

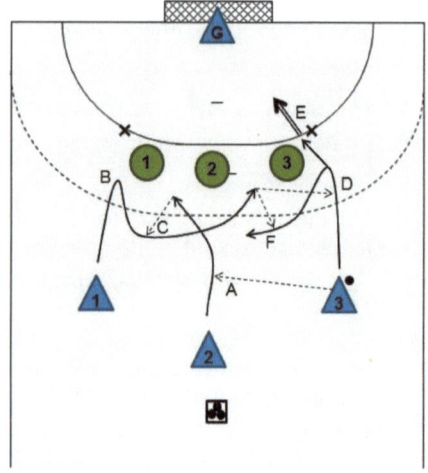

Course:

- ③ passes the ball into ②'s running path (A).
- ② makes a dynamic piston movement towards the gap between ① and ②.
- ① makes a parallel piston movement towards the left side of ① (B), takes on the crossing of ②, and receives the ball (C).
- ① dynamically dribbles across the center and makes a piston movement between ② and ③.
- ③ makes a parallel piston movement towards the right side of ③.
    - He may receive the ball from ① into his path (D) and try to break through (E)
    - Or, if ③ prevents him from breaking through, he may take on the crossing and receive the ball from ① (F).

- After he has played the pass (F), ①immediately moves back sideways to the right back position (G).
- ③ dynamically dribbles across the center and makes a piston movement between ② and ① and, if possible, tries to break through (H).
- After his initial action, ② slightly moves back to the side immediately and once again makes a parallel piston movement towards the left side of ①.
- If ① leaves a gap on the outer side (due to closing the gap on the left side during ③'s action (H)), ② receives the ball (J) and may try to break through.
- If he cannot break through, ② takes on the crossing from ③ and receives the ball (K).
- ② dynamically dribbles across the center and makes a piston movement between ② and ③ (L).
- ① makes a parallel piston movement towards the right side of ③.
    - He may receive the ball from ② into his path (M) and try to break through (E)
    - Or, if ③ prevents him from breaking through, he may take on the crossing and receive the ball from ② (N).
- And so on.

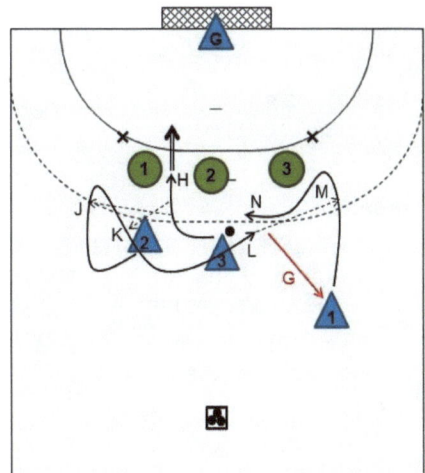

⚠ Each player should first try to break through in a highly dynamic manner. If this is not possible, they should immediately initiate a crossing at high speed and try to force their counterpart to move along.

⚠ The defensive players should interrupt the crossing movements by communicating clearly.

9. Fast throw-off/1st and 2nd wave

No. 43	Fast throw-off	8	★★
Topic:	Fast throw-off/1st and 2nd wave		
Equipment required:	1 small gym mat, 2 cones, 1 handball per player		

Course:

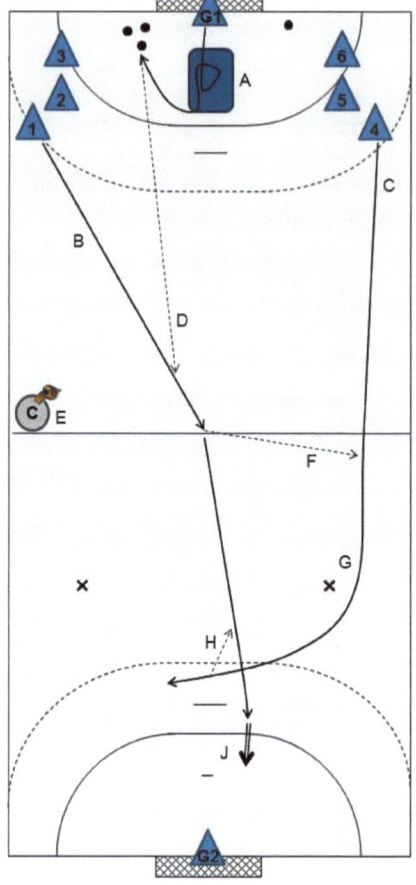

- The goalkeeper G1 starts the course and makes a somersault on the small gym mat (A).
- This is the sign for 1 and 4 to start running (B and C).
- 1 runs to the throw-off point on the center line and, once he has reached the throw-off point, receives a pass from the goalkeeper G1 (D).
- 4 should adjust his speed to stay slightly behind 1 and to keep a certain distance to the center line.
- If 1 stands at the throw-off point correctly according to the rule, the coach whistles (E).
- Now, 4 must considerably speed up and receives the ball from 1 into his running path (F).
- 4 dribbles around the cone (G), crosses 1 in the center, and passes the ball into 1's path (H).
- 1 shoots at the goal (J).
- Afterwards, 2 and 5 start the same course, etc.

⚠ The goalkeeper G1 should pass the ball to the throw-off point (D) in such a way that 1 reaches the throw-off point with one foot after 1 or 2 steps and can then pass the ball immediately after the coach has whistled.

⚠ 4 should coordinate his path towards the center line in such a way that, after the whistle, he can cross the center line at full speed (E) and receive the ball there (F).

No. 44	Coordination legwork with two subsequent 1-on-1 fast break situations	8	★★
	Topic: Fast throw-off/1st and 2nd wave		
	Equipment required: 2 hoops, 1 handball per player		

Course (figure 1):
- ▲ (with ball) and ● each stand inside a hoop.
- On command, ▲ and ● each start jumping with one foot out of their hoop and back into it again (A). They keep jumping in circles around the hoop (to the front, to the right, to the back, to the left, etc.) until the coach gives the next command.
- Now, ▲ tries to dribble (B) into the 9-meter zone as fast as possible (C) and to shoot at the goal (D).
- If ● manages to catch up with ▲ and to touch him before he has entered the 9-meter zone, ▲ must, e.g., do 10 push-ups afterwards.
- Then, it's the next two players' turn.
- Each player must do 3 to 5 courses.

Subsequent course (figure 2):
- After the 1st action, both players must enter the 9-meter zone (especially ●, if he didn't catch up with ▲).
- Now, both players start a fast break from the 9-meter zone (however, ▲ should have a small disadvantage, since he has shot a few seconds before (D)) (F).
- After the shot, the goalkeeper G fetches the ball as fast as possible (G) (put an extra ball on the floor next to the goal, just in case the other ball has rolled off too far) and plays a long pass to ● (H).
- ● shoots at the opposite goal (not shown in the figure).
- If, during the fast break, ▲ manages to touch ● before he has entered the 9-meter zone, ● must also do 10 push-ups afterwards.

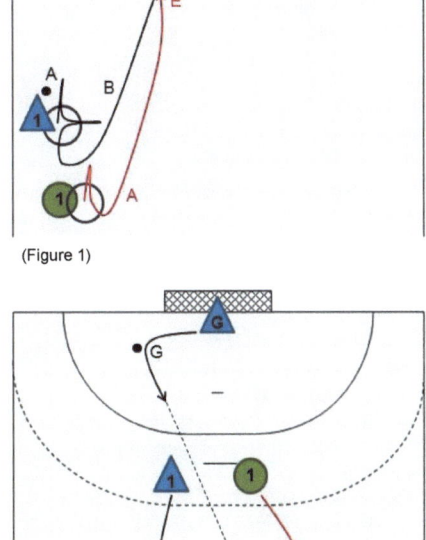

(Figure 1)

(Figure 2)

No. 45	Quick running moves with subsequent 1-on-1 fast break	8	★★

Topic:	Fast break 1st and 2nd wave
Equipment required:	6 cones, 1 ball box with sufficient number of handballs

Setting:
- Define a double-field using 6 cones (2 squared fields of 3 meters' length and 3 meters' width)

Course:
- One player per squared field. Both start on command.
- One of the players (here 1) sprints quickly from one cone of his field to the other (A). The player may choose his running path freely, however, he must not touch the same cone 2 times in a row.
- The second player (here 1) copies the running path of his teammate and runs the same path in his field (B).
- Eventually, the coach calls out "GO" while he rolls a slow ball into the other half of the court (C).
- Both players sprint towards the ball at once (D).
- The player who reaches the ball first (here 1) becomes the attacking player (E) and tries to score a goal on the other half of the court (G).
- The other player becomes the defensive player and tries to interrupt the fast break (F).
- Once the attacking player has shot or has been interrupted, the defensive player (here 1) starts to run a fast break (H), receives a pass from the goalkeeper (who has quickly secured the ball or picked up the extra ball next to the goal (J)) (K), and eventually shoots at the goal (L).
- Afterwards, two new players start the course.

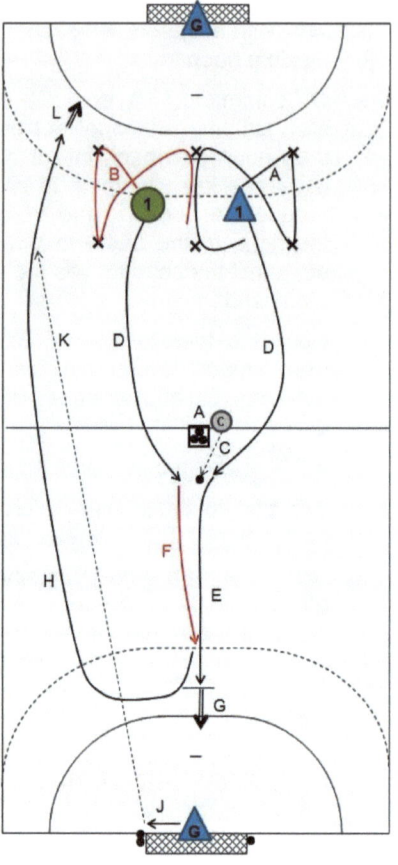

⚠ The players must switch from the running exercise to the fast break immediately (D).

⚠ After the first shot (G), the defensive player must adjust to the new situation immediately and start the fast break to the other side at once (H).

⚠ Switch the goalkeepers at regular intervals.

No. 46		2ⁿᵈ wave – Initiation	12	★★
	Topic:	Fast break, 1ˢᵗ and 2ⁿᵈ wave		
	Equipment required:	2 cones, sufficient number of handballs		

Course:

- 1, 2, and 3 start the 2ⁿᵈ wave and try to break through 1 and 2 (A) and to shoot at the goal (B).
- Immediately afterwards, 1 and 2 (D) initiate the 2ⁿᵈ wave together with 4, who throws in a new ball (C). Now, they try to break through 3 and 4 and to shoot at the goal.
- Two players of the first group (1, 2, and 3) become the new defensive players.
- After the action of 1, 2, and 4, 3, 4, and 5 start their action.
- And so on.

⚠ The players should play the 2ⁿᵈ wave at high speed.

⚠ The defensive players should change their actions frequently (defensive, offensive).

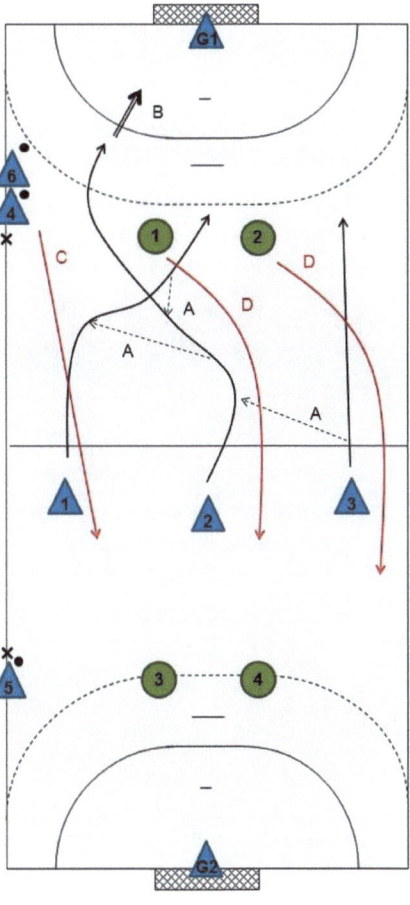

Variant: Fixed initiation

- ▲2 passes the ball into ▲1's running path (A).
- ▲1 dribbles dynamically to the right side, forces ●2 to move along with him, and crosses ▲3 (D).
- ⚠ ▲3 must start dynamically from the far right!
- ▲2 simultaneously moves to the left and takes over ▲1's position (C).
- ▲3 moves dynamically towards the gap between ●1 and ●2 and tries to break through. If ▲3 is successful, he shoots at the goal.
- If ●1 and ●2 manage to close the gap (G) and to prevent ▲3 from shooting, ▲3 passes the ball into ▲2's running path (E) who then shoots (F).
- Immediately afterwards, ●1 and ●2 start over together with ▲4 and repeat the course on the other side.

⚠ Make sure the players cross dynamically at full speed.

⚠ The players must switch quickly from defense to offense and vice versa.

No. 47	Fast break competition	8	★★
	Topic: Fast break, 1st and 2nd wave		
Equipment required:	6 cones, 1 ball per player		

Basic course:
- Make 2 teams.
- 2 players (one player of each team) do the course.
- The other players jog at relaxed pace around the cones in the center (A).

Course:
- 1 and 2 stand on the wing position and start to run a fast break simultaneously.
- The goalkeepers each play a long pass (B).
- 1 and 2 each shoot at the goal (C).
- After they have shot, both players sprint to the goal and touch one of the goalposts (D).
- Afterwards, they start a second fast break, receive a long pass from the respective goalkeeper into their running path (E), and eventually shoot at the goal (F).
- The player who shot the most goals, scores for his team. If there is a tie, both teams score.
- 1 and 2 then join the jogging players in the center. Two new players start the same course.
- Each player must do the course 2 times (i.e. shoot 4 times); the final score will be settled at the end. The losing team must do push-ups or sit-ups, for example.
- After a short break, the second course starts.

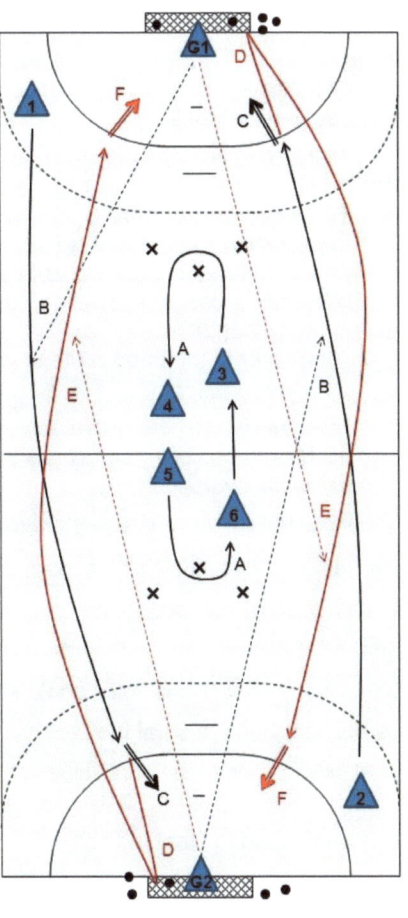

2nd course:
- Each player must do the course 3 times (i.e. shoot 6 times).
- After a short break, further courses may be started.

10. Defensive action

No. 48	Stealing the ball	8	★
Topic:	Defensive action		
Equipment required:	1 handball per team of 2		

Setting:
- The players form pairs; each pair has one handball.

Course 1:
- The player in the front (1) starts to walk slowly and dribbles the ball with one hand in front of his body (A) (he must not change the dribbling hand).
- The player in the back starts to jog slowly (A), overtakes 1 on the side on which the other player dribbles the ball (B), and steals the ball while overtaking (C).

⚠️ 1 should use the hand that is closer to 1 to steal the ball (i.e. he must not lean over to the other side!). If 1 overtakes 1 on the left side (1 dribbles the ball with his left hand), 1 uses his right hand to steal the ball; if 1 overtakes 1 on the right side (1 dribbles the ball with his right hand), 1 uses his left hand to steal the ball.

⚠️ When 1 tries to steal the ball, he must adjust his timing, i.e. the ball must bounce back up from the floor as he tries to steal it.

- Once 1 has overtaken 1, he stops and starts to dribble himself (D).
- The course starts over; this time, however, 1 tries to steal the ball (E and F).
- And so on.

Course 2:
- This time, 1 jogs slowly while he dribbles.

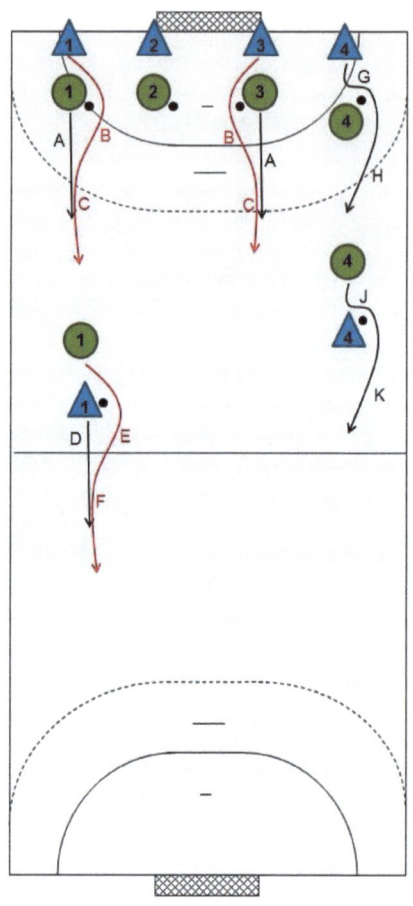

Course 3:
- Both players stand face-to-face.
- ④ dribbles the ball in front of his body while standing on the spot.
- ▲ should wait for the right moment (when the ball bounces back up from the floor), then quickly make a step forward, and eventually steal the ball (G).
- ▲, who now has the ball, jogs a few meters (H) and then turns around. The course starts over; this time, however, ④ tries to steal the ball from ▲ (J and K).

No. 49	Basic practice: Step out and secure	9 (11)	★
	Topic: Defensive action		
Equipment required:	1 handball		

Setting:
- Draw a circle on the court floor or use an already existing circle.

Course:
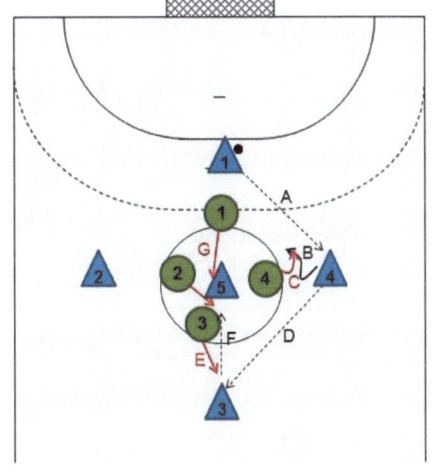

- By playing quick passes (A and D), the attacking players ▲1, ▲2, ▲3, and ▲4 either try to enter the circle with the ball (B) or to pass to ▲5 who is standing in the center of the circle (F). If they are successful, the attacking players score.
- The defensive players ●1, ●2, ●3 and ●4 must actively step towards the player who is in ball possession (C and E) in order to prevent him from entering the circle.
- The defensive players who are not close to the player in ball possession must step back into the circle in order to cover the player inside the circle (G).
- The attacking players play 15 attacks; afterwards, they switch tasks (one of the attacking players stays in the center of the circle). Which team scores highest?

⚠ The defensive players must communicate: Who makes a step forward towards the attacking player? Who covers the player in the circle? Etc.

⚠ The defensive players must actively step towards the respective attacking players in order to prevent them from entering the circle and to make it harder for them to pass the ball to their teammates inside and outside the circle.

No. 50	1-on-1 play with subsequent action for the attacking player	8	★
Topic:	Defensive action		
Equipment required:	6 cones, 1 ball box with sufficient number of handballs		

Setting:
- Define a narrow corridor for the defensive action using cones. The aim is to simulate a direct 1-on-1 play with little space for the attacking player.

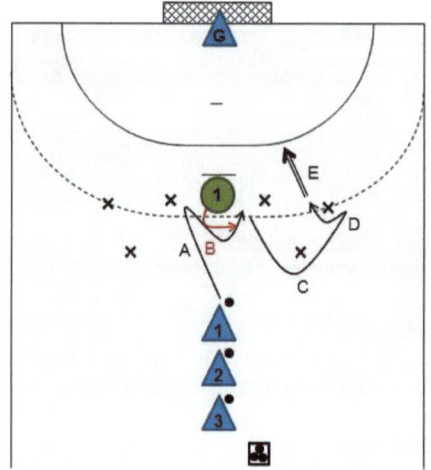

Course:
- ▲1 starts with the ball, passes it to ●1, and receives a return pass into his piston movement path (not shown in the figure).
- ▲1 moves forward, then plays 1-on-1 against ●1 within the space defined by the cones, and tries to break through (A).
- If ▲1 manages to break through within the space between the cones, he may shoot at the goal.
- If ▲1 is tackled or pushed out of the space defined by the cones, ▲1 immediately moves back to the backmost cone (C), dynamically dribbles forward, makes an extensive running feint (D) in front of the cone and eventually a jump shot once he is line with the cone (E).
- As soon as ▲1 has finished his 1-on-1 play against ●1, ▲2 immediately starts his action.

Basic course:
- Each defensive player defends 8 to 12 attacks in a row (high intensity); afterwards, change the defensive player until every player has played defense once.

⚠ By doing quick steps and using his arms, ●1 must try to tackle ▲1 or push him out of the space between the cones/block him (B) in order to prevent ▲1 from shooting.

⚠ If ▲1 is pushed out to the right side, the subsequent action takes place on the right side (C, D, and E); if he is pushed out to the left side, the subsequent action takes place on the left side.

No. 51	1-on-1 offense and defense switching	10	★★
	Topic: Defensive action		
	Equipment required: 8 cones, 2 balls per group of 8		

Course:

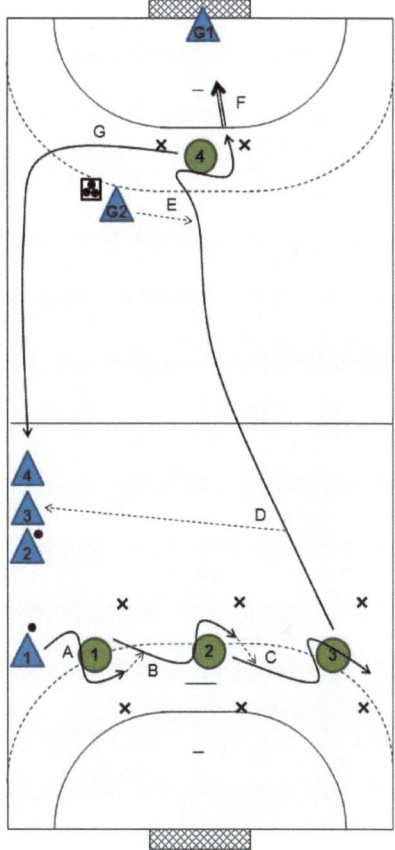

- ① starts the course by passing the ball to ①, then starts to run, receives a return pass, and eventually plays 1-on-1 against ① (A). ① must try to prevent ① from breaking through the cones.
- Afterwards, ① passes the ball to ①; ① becomes the new defensive player.
- ① passes the ball to ②, receives a return pass into his running path, and plays 1-on-1 against ② (B).
- ② passes the ball to ③, receives a return pass into his running path, and plays 1-on-1 against ③ (C).
- ② passes the ball into the running path of ③ who starts to run a fast break and then passes the ball to one of the attacking players without the ball (here ③) (D).
- Then, ③ keeps running, receives a pass from the 2nd goalkeeper into his running path (E), plays 1- on-1 against ④, and eventually shoots at the goal (F).
- Afterwards, ④ starts immediately and runs at high speed into the other half of the court. Once he has arrived, he lines up again (G). ③ takes over the position of ④.

⚠ The defensive players should prevent a break-through by making quick steps and using their arms; they must act in a highly dynamic manner.

Basic course:

- As soon as ② has finished his action against ③ (C), ② starts his action against ①, etc.

No. 52	Intensive continuous defense and offense switching with subsequent action	8	★★★
Topic:	Defensive action		
Equipment required:	10 cones, 1 ball box with sufficient number of handballs		

Course:

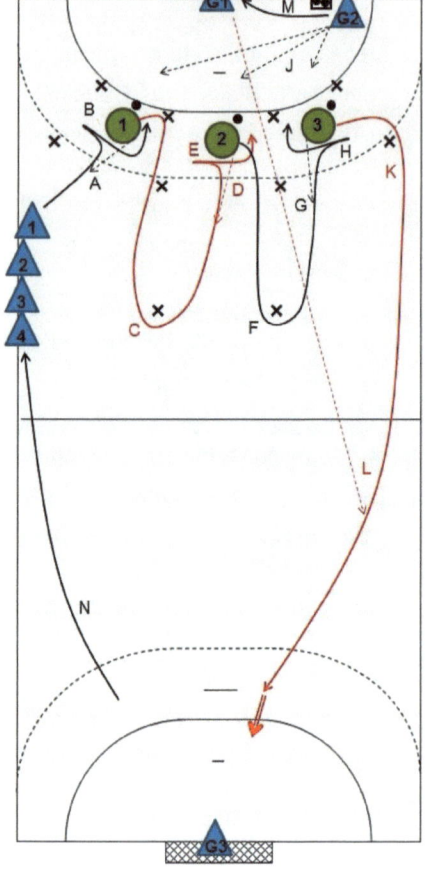

- 🔵1 starts to run and receives a pass from 🟢1 into his running path (A).
- 🔵1 plays 1-on-1 against 🟢1 and tries to shoot at the goal (B).
- Following the action (B), 🔵1 picks up a new ball and becomes the new defensive player.
- Afterwards, 🟢1 starts to sprint immediately, runs around the cone (C), receives a pass from 🟢2 into his path (D), and then plays 1-on-1 against 🟢2 (E).
- After the action (E), 🟢1 picks up a new ball and becomes the new defensive player.
- Afterwards, 🟢2 starts to sprint immediately, runs around the cone (F), receives a pass from 🟢3 into his path (G), and then plays 1-on-1 against 🟢3 (H).
- Following the action, 🟢3 starts to sprint immediately, runs around the cone (K), receives a pass from the goalkeeper G1 into his path (L), and eventually shoots at the opposite goal.
  Afterwards, 🟢3 lines up again (N).
- After the action (E), 🟢2 picks up a new ball and becomes the new defensive player.
- As soon as 🟢3 has started to run the fast break, the goalkeepers switch tasks; G2 plays in the goal while G1 feeds the defensive players with new handballs.
- Once G2 stands in the goal, 🟢2 starts his 1-on-1 play against 🔵1, etc.
- Repeat until each player has run the course 1 to 2 times.

From warm-up to handball team play
75 exercises for every handball training

Basic course:
- If there are not enough handballs available for the new defensive players, the goalkeeper G2 passes a ball (J).

⚠ The defensive players must adjust immediately after the defensive play and start the next action (C, F, and K).

No. 53	Intensive continuous 1-on-1 defense and offense play after previous exertion	8	★★★
Topic:	Defensive action		
Equipment required:	6 cones, 3 small gym mats, 1 ball box with sufficient number of handballs		

Basic course:
- Depending on his level of performance, 1 does 1 to 2 courses (i.e. 1 to 2 times nine 1-on-1 situations in a row).
- The two cones in the back, around which the players must run after the action, should be positioned in such a way that 1, 2, and 3 do not have to wait for too long until they do the course on the next position. They should continue as soon as they have run around the cone.
- The space between the cones for the 1-on-1 play should be rather narrow so that the defensive player has a chance to prevent the attacking player from breaking through – even at the end of the exercise, when he might already be exhausted.
- 5 and 6 (and the remaining players) fetch the balls that have been shot at the goal so that the attacking players can be fed adequately.

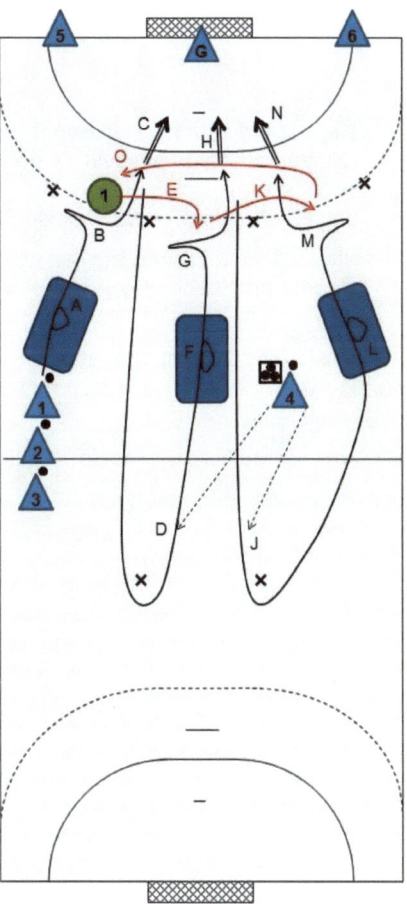

Course:

- ① does a somersault on the small gym mat while holding the ball in his hands (A), passes the ball to ①, receives a return pass, and then plays 1-on-1 against ① (B) in order to break though and shoot at the goal (C).
- ② must time his start so that ① is able to position himself correctly after the previous action, etc.
- After the shot, ① sprints around the cone and receives a new ball from ④ (D).
- As soon as ③ has finished his 1-on-1 play, ① changes the defensive position (E). After he has done a somersault in the center (F), ① plays 1-on-1 against ① (G) in order to break through and shoot at the goal (H).
- Once again, ② and ③ each start delayed (as before).
- After the actions, ①, ②, and ③ sprint around the cone again (J) and ① changes the defensive position (K).
- Repeat the course on the right back position (L, M, and N).
- Depending on their level of performance, the four players do the course a second time, starting from the left side (O). Alternatively, a new defensive player and three new attacking players start the same course immediately after ③ has finished the last action on the right side.
- Repeat until each player has played the defense course once.

⚠ ① should prevent the attacking player from breaking through in a highly dynamic manner and actively step forward towards him.

⚠ Give ① sufficient time to position himself correctly for the next defensive action. However, ① must not take a break between the individual actions.

No. 54	2-on-2 continuous defense switching with additional exercise	8	★★
Topic:	Defensive action		
Equipment required:	7 cones, 1 ball per group of 8		

Setting:
- Define three target areas using cones ("cone goals").
- Position 1 cone in the center of the playing field.

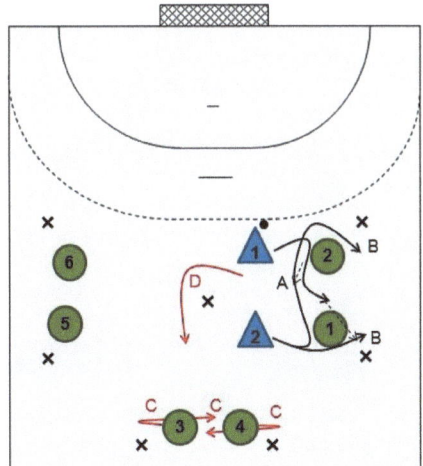

Course:
- 🔺1 and 🔺2 play 2-on-2 against 🔵1 and 🔵2.
- By crossing (A) and simple breaking through (B), 🔺1 and 🔺2 try to position one player with a ball on the line between both cones.
- The defense players must defend the cone goal dynamically and communicate clearly (take over /hand over) in order to prevent the attacking players from breaking through (C). If the defensive players manage to tackle the attacking players or to push them out of the playing field, they get a point whereas the attacking players get a penalty point. If the attacking players manage to break through, the points are distributed vice versa.
- Afterwards, 🔵1 and 🔵2 immediately start a counter movement, run around the cone in the center (D), and eventually play 2-on-2 against 🟢3 and 🟢4.
- The points are distributed as before. The teams must do 5 push-ups per penalty point, e.g. Each team may get a maximum of 2 penalty points (2 actions in total; 1 offensive and 1 defensive action). If the team has neither points nor penalty points (i.e. no points at all) or 2 points, they do not have to do the additional exercise.
- Afterwards, 🟢3 and 🟢4 play 2-on-2 against 🟢5 and 🟢6. Then, 🟢5 and 🟢6 play 2-on-2 against 🔺1 and 🔺2, etc.

⚠️ The two defensive players should act against the attacking players in a highly dynamic manner and organize the hand over/take over by communicating clearly.

Intermediate exercise after the two subsequent actions
(1 defensive play and 1 offensive play)

- First, the players must do their push-ups, if applicable.
- Both players stand next to a cone and start to jump with one leg quickly on the spot (E).
    - to the left of
    - in front of
    - to the right of
    - and finally behind

  an imaginary line on the floor.
- After the last jump, the players immediately start to sidestep dynamically towards the opposite cone (F), touch it, and dynamically run back to the starting point at once (G).

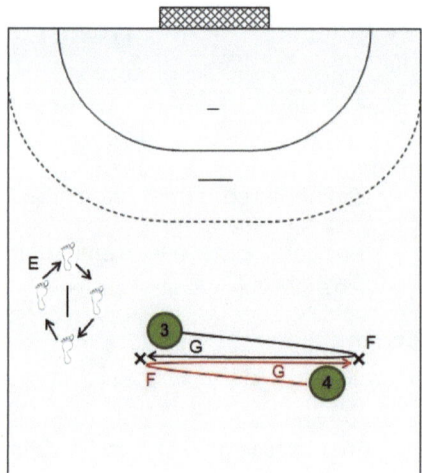

- Afterwards, ③ and ④ wait until it is their turn again to play defense 2-on-2.
- And so on.

No. 55	Middle block pivot hand-over and take-over	8	★★
	Topic: Defensive action		
	Equipment required: 2 cones, 1 ball box with sufficient number of handballs		

Basic course:

- 6 stands next to the 7-meter line, not moving!

Course:

- 1 starts a piston movement and receives a pass from 2 into his running path (A).
- 1 actively steps forward into the piston movement path of 1 (B) and attacks 1 offensively.
- 2 moves towards the center and tries to cover 6 so that he cannot receive the ball from 1 (C).
- During the 1-on-1 play against 1, 1 moves towards the center and passes the ball to 2 (D).
- 2 makes a quick piston movement and passes the ball further into the piston movement path of 3 (E).
- 1 moves towards the center and tries to cover 6 so that he cannot receive the ball from 3 (F).
- 2 actively steps forward into the piston movement path of 3 (G) and attacks 3 offensively.
- During the 1-on-1 play against 2, 3 moves towards the center and passes the ball to 2 (H).
- 2 passes the ball back to 1 and the course starts over.

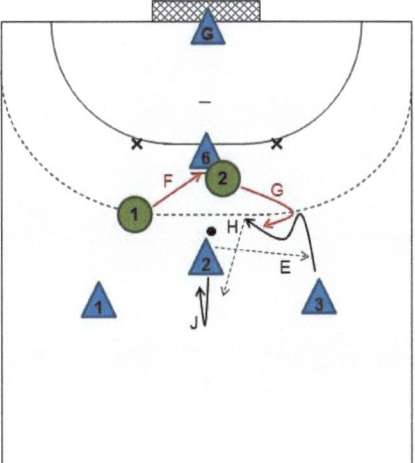

Extension:

- During the team play with 2, 1 and 3 may play 10 passes only until they must play a pass to the pivot 6 (K).
- However, 6 still must not move; he is allowed to stretch towards the ball with his upper body and arms only.

⚠ 1 and 2 should step forward towards the attacking players offensively and try to interrupt the attacking players' actions within the 9-meter zone actively and intensively.

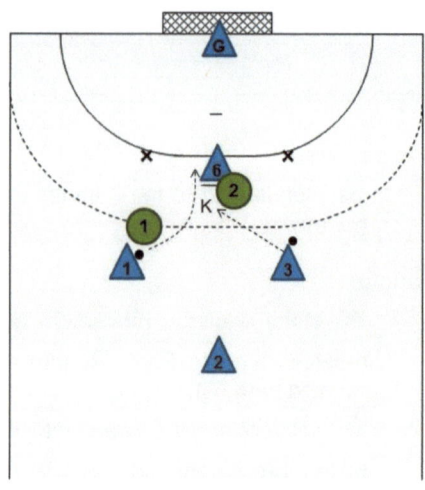

From warm-up to handball team play
75 exercises for every handball training

No. 56	Goal corner switching between defense players and goalkeeper	8	★★★
	Topic: Defensive action		
	Equipment required: 2 cones, 2 ball boxes with sufficient number of handballs		

Objective:
- Make the skillful back position player shoot at the "intended" corner of the goal.

Basic course:
- 2, 3, 4, and 6 play 4-on-4 against 2, 3, 4, and 5.
- The four attacking players play the attacking strategies below in order to score goals.
- Once they have played five attacks, the attacking players and the defensive players switch positions. Which team scores highest when playing five attacks?

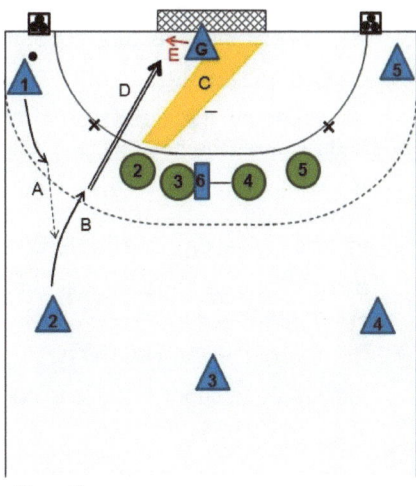

(Figure 1)

Strategy 1 (figure 1):
- 1 starts the piston movement on the wing position and passes the ball into the running path of 2 (A).
- 2 makes a piston movement towards the outer side (B); in this situation, the defensive players should communicate as usual. 2 covers the long corner (C), forcing 2 to shoot at the short corner of the goal (D and E).

⚠ The defensive players must communicate clearly in order to cover the pivot.

Strategy 2 (figure 2):
- If 2 moves through the center after the initial pass from 1 (F), the defensive players and the goalkeeper G switch corners.
- Now, 2 covers the short corner (G) and the goalkeeper G covers the long corner, forcing 2 to shoot at the long corner of the goal (H and J).

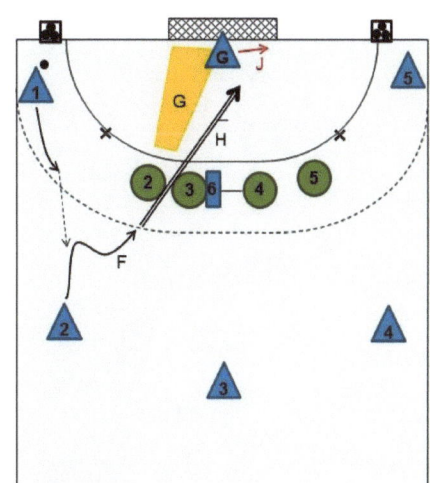

(Figure 2)

Strategy 3 (figure 3):

- 5 starts the piston movement on the wing position and passes into the piston movement path of 4 (K).
- 4 passes into the running path of 3 to the left (L).
- 2 takes on the crossing of 3 and receives the ball (M).
- 2 approaches the goal dynamically (N).
- In this situation, the defensive players and the goalkeeper G switch corners as well.
- 3 covers the short corner (O), forcing 2 to shoot in the long corner of the goal (P and R).

(Figure 3)

No. 57	Outnumbered middle block defense	10	★★
	Topic: Defensive action		
	Equipment required: 2 cones, 2 tape strips, 1 ball		

Basic course:

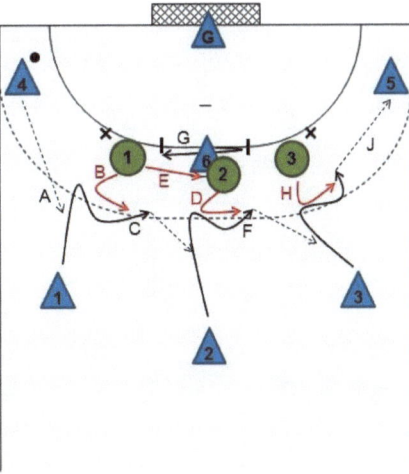

- 6 may move within the area defined by the tape strips (G).
- 4 and 5 serve as receivers.
- The attacking players may play a maximum of 12 passes per attack, then they must shoot at the goal.
- The main task of 1, 2, and 3 during their team play actions is to pass the ball to 6. If the defensive players do not act offensively, the attacking players may shoot from the 9-meter zone or try to break through and shoot from the 6-meter line.
- The players switch positions after five attacks. Which team defends best?

Course:

- 1 receives a pass from 4 into his running path (A).
- 1 should offensively step forward towards the piston movement path of 1 (B) and actively try to interrupt 1.
- 1 passes the ball into the piston movement path of 2 (C).
- 2 should offensively step forward towards the piston movement path of 2 (D) and actively try to interrupt 2.
- 1 moves towards the center and covers 6 (E).
- 2 passes the ball into the piston movement path of 3 (F).
- 3 should offensively step forward towards the piston movement path of 3 (H) and actively try to interrupt 3.
- 3 passes the ball to the wing position to 5 (J); then the course starts over from the other side, etc.

Allocations:
- ①, ②, and ③ should keep calling out who is in charge of covering .

LB is in ball possession:

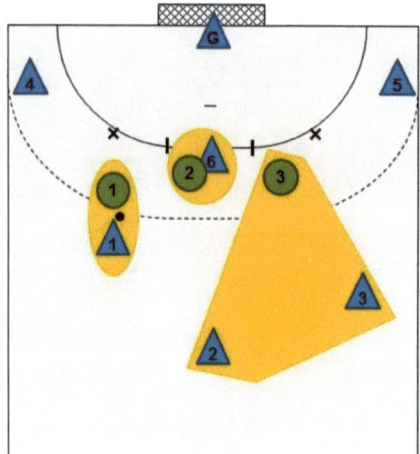

CB is in ball possession:

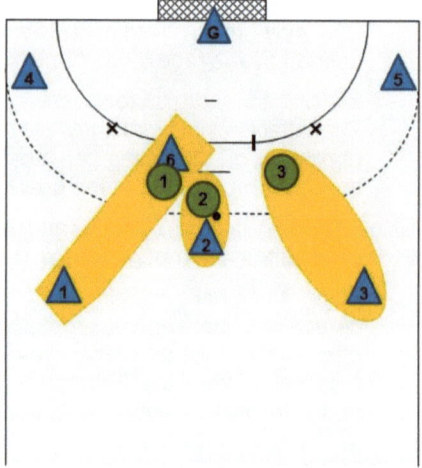

RB is in ball possession:

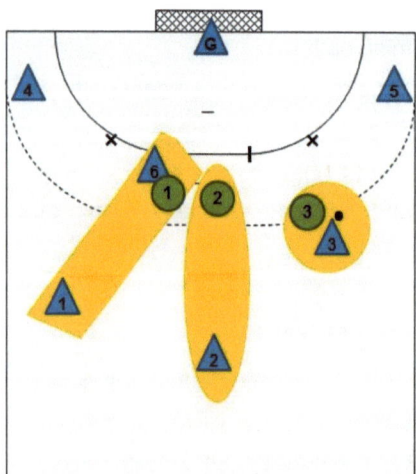

No. 58	4-on-4 defensive action with subsequent fast break on the wing positions	14	★★
	Topic: Defensive action		
	Equipment required: 4 cones, sufficient number of handballs		

Basic setting:

- 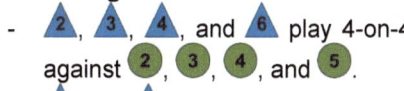 2, 3, 4, and 6 play 4-on-4 against 2, 3, 4, and 5.
- 1 and 5 serve as receivers.

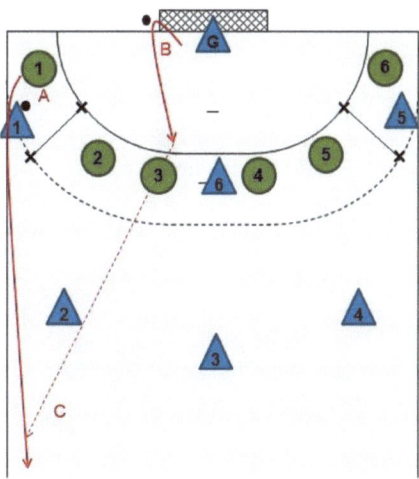

Course:

- 2, 3, 4, and 6 should try to shoot at the goal while playing freely.
- 2, 3, 4, and 5 move forward and to the side aggressively. The defensive players must communicate clearly when handing over 6.
- As soon as the attacking players approach the goal in the final action, 1 and 6 start to run a fast break (A).
- The goalkeeper fetches the ball quickly (B) and initiates the fast break with a long pass (C).
- 1 or 6 eventually finish the fast break by shooting at the opposite goal (2nd goalkeeper); afterwards, both run back quickly.
- If the defensive players manage to steal the ball, or if the attacking players miss the goal, the defensive players score. If one of the players running the fast break shoots a goal, the defensive players score again. If the attacking players shoot a goal, they score.
- The defensive players and the attacking players switch tasks after each attack.

Objective:

- Which team is the first to score 10 times?
- The losing team must do push-ups or sit-ups.

⚠ Both wing players must start the fast break early, i.e. during the final action of the attacking players.

⚠ The defensive players should move forward and to the side in a highly dynamic manner and maintain the correct defense posture (throwing hand/hip).

11. Closing games

No. 59	4-on-4 with quick offense / defense switching	8	★★
	Topic: Closing games		
Equipment required:	4 small gym mats, 1 handball		

Course:

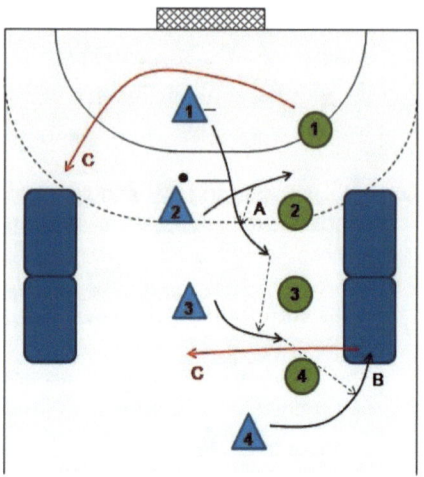

- 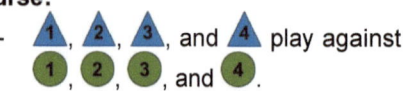 play against ①, ②, ③, and ④.
- By means of simple crossing and parallel piston movement (1-on-1 actions), the team in ball possession must try to lay down the ball on their opponents' gym mats (A and B).
- The defensive team defends their mats and tries to prevent the attacking players from laying down the ball. If they manage to steal the ball, or if the attacking players manage to lay down the ball on a mat, both teams switch tasks immediately (C).

Methodological course:
- During the 1st third, the attacking players must try to break through 1-on-1. If they are successful, they get two points.
- During the 2nd third, the attacking players must try to approach the mat by crossing (in this situation, crossing is mandatory).
- During the 3rd third, the attacking players may play completely free.

Playing time:
- Three times 5 minutes with short breaks in between.

The losing team must do push-ups or sit-ups, e.g., after the respective third.

⚠ The defensive players should try to stand closely together and keep the attacking players in front of them.

⚠ The defensive players must prevent the attacking players, both with and without the ball, from breaking through.

⚠ The players must rapidly switch from offense to defense and vice versa.

No. 60	**Fast throw-off and 2nd wave switch game**	12	★★
	Topic: Closing games		
Equipment required:	4 cones, sufficient number of handballs		

Course:

- ① receives a pass from ② into his running path (A).
- ③ runs a curve to the outer side dynamically, then runs dynamically to the inner side while taking on the crossing of ①, and eventually receives the ball (B).
- ① and ② should act offensively and variably and put ③ under pressure to make a decision.
    - If ② steps forward offensively, he may play to the pivot ⑥ (C).
    - If ② does not consequently step forward towards ③, he may try to shoot or break through himself (D).
    - If ① helps out, ③ may interact with ②, who then breaks through or makes a jump shot at the goal (E).

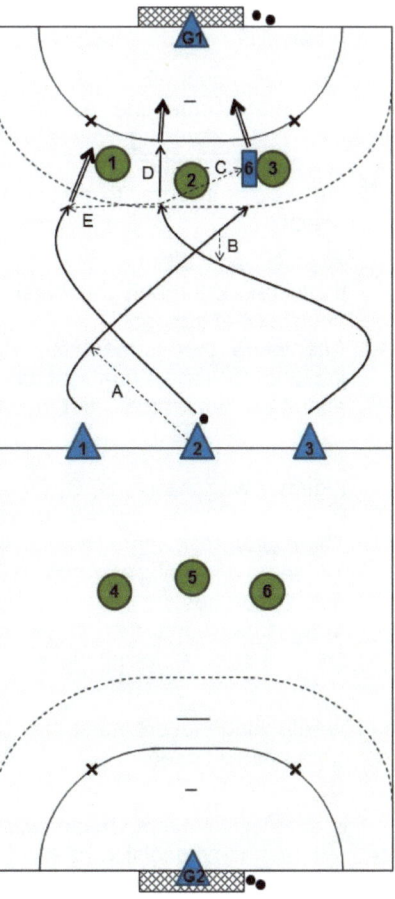

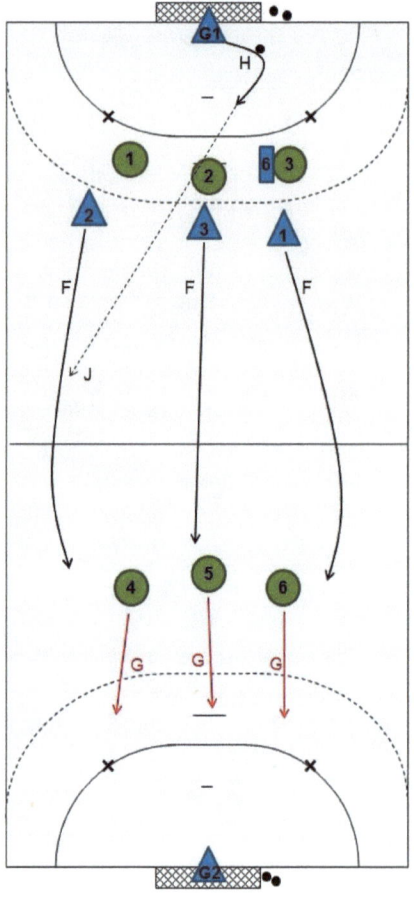

- Afterwards, 1, 2, and 3 immediately start the next action (1, 2, 3, and 6 keep their positions and wait for the third action). 1, 2, and 3 run a fast break (F).
- 4, 5, and 6 wait closely behind the center line. As soon as the first attacking player has crossed the center line, they may move back in order to defend the attack (G).
- 1, 2, and 3 may play freely, try to break through the defense, and shoot at the goal.
- Afterwards, they immediately start the third action, run a fast break and then repeat the first course against 1, 2, and 3 playing together with 6 (A, B, C, D, and E).
- The players can score three times; for each goal missed, they must do 10 push-ups.
- Afterwards, repeat the course with the next three attacking players.

⚠ The attacking players must play the three attacks at full speed.

⚠ The defensive players should increase the pressure on the attacking players and force them to make a decision by suddenly covering one of them.

⚠ The goalkeepers should put some extra balls next to their goals in order to keep the game going (H).

Variant:
- The attacking players must play five attacks in a row.

No. 61	Simple 4-on-4 switch game	14	★
Topic:	Closing games		
Equipment required:	1 handball		

Course:

- 1, 2, 3, and 4 play 4-on-4 against 1, 2, 3, and 4.
- As soon as the attack is over, 1, 2, 3, and 4 start a quick counter attack on the other half of the court and play against 1, 2, 3, and 4 who should start their defensive play far off the 9-meter line.
- After the attack, 1, 2, 3, and 4 immediately become the new defensive players (defensive play far off the 9-meter line).
- If a team scores, the goalkeeper immediately starts over by playing a pass; there is no throw-off at the center line.
- Which team has scored highest after 10 minutes? Define exercises for the second and third place before starting a game.

⚠ The teams should play their counter attacks quickly from one side to the other. Breaks should be avoided.

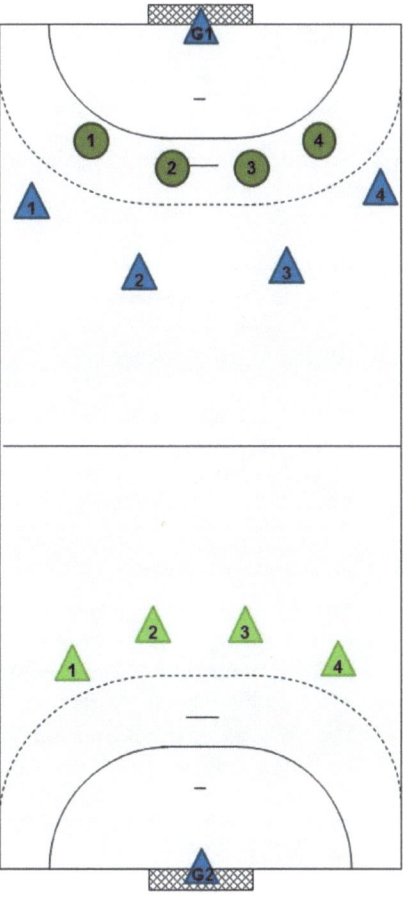

No. 62	Intensive 4-on-4 switch game	10	★★
Topic:	Closing games		
Equipment required:	2 ball boxes with sufficient number of handballs		

Basic course:
- Make 2 to 3 teams of four.
- 1, 2, 3, and 4 play 4-on-4 against 1, 2, 3, and 4.
- During an attack, each team may play no more than 6 passes, beginning at the center line. After they have played the 6 passes, they must shoot at the goal.
- Free 4-on-4 play.
- After 4 to 5 minutes, the "winning team" may take a break and the waiting team's turn begins.

Course:
- If the attacking players manage to shoot at the goal after they have played 6 passes or less, and if they score a goal, they receive a point.
- Afterwards, the tasks are switched immediately. However, 1, 2, 3, and 4 (the former attacking players) must step on the 6-meter line with one foot (A). Only then they are allowed to interrupt the new attacking players (B).
- 1, 2, 3, and 4 now become the attacking players; however, they must all step on the goal line with one foot before they are allowed to start their attack (C).

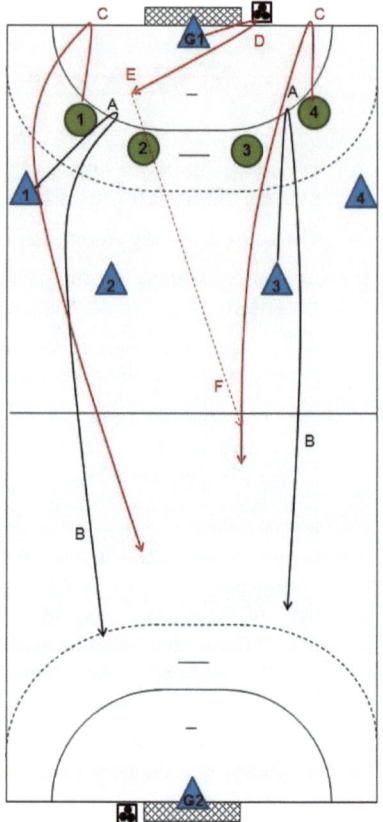

- After the shot, the goalkeeper G1 must run to the ball box, fetch a new ball (D), and change his position (E) in such a way that he can play a diagonal pass to the attacking player (F).
- Afterwards, repeat the course on the other side, etc.

⚠ After 2 to 3 courses, individual players may not be able to keep up anymore, i.e. they are not fast enough when it comes to stepping on the respective lines. However, they always have to step on the line! G1 and G2 may have to wait a little until they pass the ball again (F).

⚠ If a team does not manage to shoot at the goal after they have played 6 passes, the coach whistles and the attacking player must pass the ball to the opponents' goalkeeper immediately. Afterwards, the players must run to their line and the game continues as usual.

12. Endurance

No. 63	Piston movement and passing with additional running paths and under time pressure	10	★
	Topic: Endurance		
Equipment required:	4 cones, 1 handball		

Basic course:
- Make two teams of five.
- Measure how long it takes the two teams to complete two courses (1 to 5 and back to 1; afterwards, the second course begins).

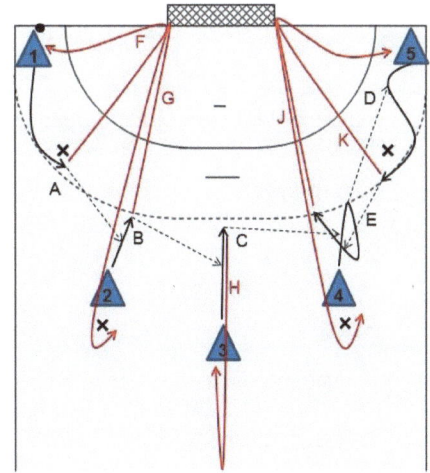

Course:
- 1 makes a piston movement around the cone on a curved path and passes the ball into the piston movement path of 2 (A).
- 2 makes a dynamic piston movement forward and passes the ball into the piston movement path of 3 (B).
- 3 makes a dynamic piston movement forward and passes the ball into the piston movement path of 4 (C).
- 4 makes a piston movement slightly towards the right side and passes the ball into the path of 5 towards the goal (D).
- 5 makes a dynamic piston movement around the cone on a curved path and passes the ball into the piston movement path of 4 (E), etc.

Course after the pass:
- 1 must run around the cone when making the piston movement, then sprint to the goal, touch the goalpost, and go back to his initial position (F).
- If 2 and 4 receive the ball from the wing positions (1 and 5), they pass the ball to 3, sprint to the goal, touch the goalpost, and run around the backmost cone (G and J).
  ⚠ When 3 passes the ball, 2 and 4 keep their positions.
- Every time he has passed the ball (to 2 or 4), 3 sprints to the center line and back to his initial position (H).

⚠ Make sure that the players make the correct running moves during the piston movement.

⚠ Adjust the cone position to the players' level of performance.

From warm-up to handball team play
75 exercises for every handball training

No. 64	**Ball familiarization exercise focusing on running**	8	★★
	Topic: Endurance		
	Equipment required: 10 cones, 3 handballs		

Course of the inner group (1, 3, ..., and 2, 4, ...):

- 1 makes a dynamic piston movement forward (A) and passes the ball into the piston movement path (B) of 2.
- 2 passes the ball to 3 (C), also while making the piston movement, etc.

Course after the piston movement:

- 1 sidesteps to the far left (D), turns around, and sprints around the backmost cone (E).
- 1 sprints on a long straight line (F), runs around the cone on the other side, and lines up with the other group (G).
- And so on.

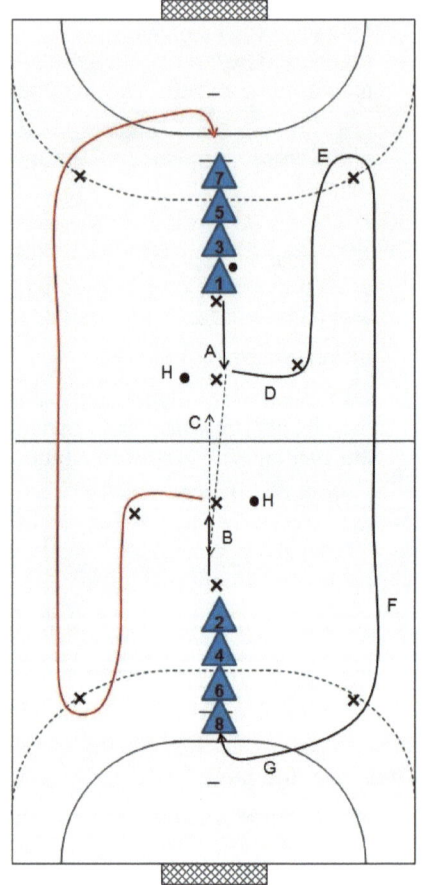

Time:
- The players have to do the exercise for about five minutes.
- Count each time a player drops the ball.
- After five minutes, the players must do, e.g., three push-ups and three sit-ups per ball drop (five bad passes/passes not caught = 15 push-ups and 15 sit-ups).
- Afterwards, the players may take a short break and then repeat the course.

⚠ The players should time their piston movements and their passes (A, B, and C) in such a way that they keep moving constantly (i.e. that they do not have to stop their movement when passing to the other group).

⚠ Adjust the distance of the cones on the side to the team's level of performance so that they can run the course smoothly and (preferably) receive the next pass (A, B, and C) immediately after they have lined up (G).

⚠ Since the players must run a lot, the exercise is very exhausting.

From warm-up to handball team play
75 exercises for every handball training

No. 65	Outdoor endurance competition on the cinder tracks	9	★★
	Topic: Endurance		
Equipment required:	1 medicine ball per group of 3		

Setting:
- Make teams of three. Each team has a medicine ball and the players stand as shown in the figure.
- Each team has a separate running track.
- Define two start lines with a distance of about 25 to 30 meters.

Course:
- On command, 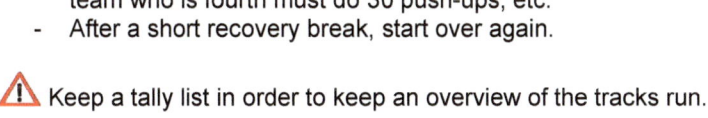 start simultaneously and sprint along their respective running track holding the medicine ball in their hands (A).
- Once they have arrived on the other side and crossed the line, they hand over the medicine ball to the next player (B).
- These players now sprint back and hand over the medicine ball to the next player (C).
- Repeat the course 30 times in total, so that each player has sprinted along the track 10 times.

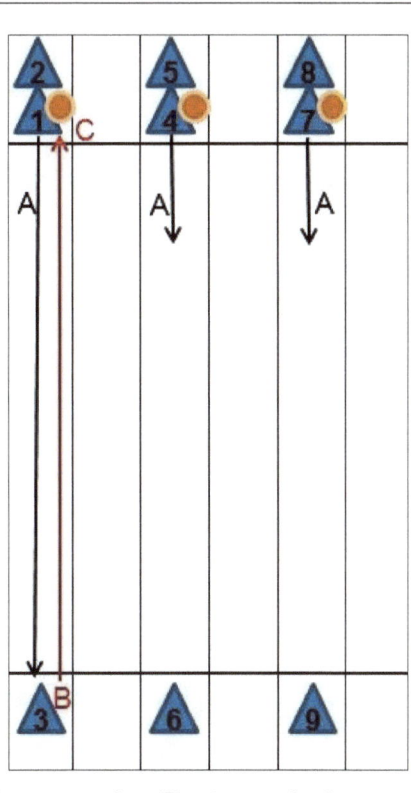

- The winning team does not have to do an exercise. The team who is second must do 10 push-ups, e.g., the team who is third must do 20 push-ups, the team who is fourth must do 30 push-ups, etc.
- After a short recovery break, start over again.

⚠ Keep a tally list in order to keep an overview of the tracks run.

No. 66	**Continuous fast break with subsequent athletics course**	8	★★★
Topic:	Endurance		
Equipment required:	1 handball per player, 2 cones, 1 large vaulting box, 1 balance bench, 1 small gym mat		

Basic course:
- The players first run their fast breaks and afterwards do the drill on the side of the court.
- Each player must do the exercise 5 times.

Course:
- 1 starts a fast break without a ball (A), receives a pass from the goalkeeper G1 into his running path (B), and shoots at the opposite goal (C).
- Afterwards, 1 starts the second fast break immediately (D), receives a pass from the goalkeeper G2 into his running path (E), and shoots at the goal (F).
- Afterwards, 1 starts the course two more times (four fast breaks in total) (G).
- After the fourth fast break, 1 runs to the side and does the individual exercises:
  - 1 does 10 push-ups for each shot that missed the goal during the fast break exercise (H).
  - On the gym mat, 1 does 10 sit-ups (J).
  - 1 lies face-down on the balance bench and pulls himself to the other side. 1 turns around and pulls himself back. He repeats this exercise one more time (he must pull himself across the bench 4 times) (K).
  - 1 jumps back and forth over the large vaulting box 5 times so that he has jumped 10 times in total (L).
  - Afterwards, 1 runs back to the start point and runs the fast breaks as soon as it is his turn again (M).
- As soon as 1 has finished his fast breaks, 2 starts the same course, etc.

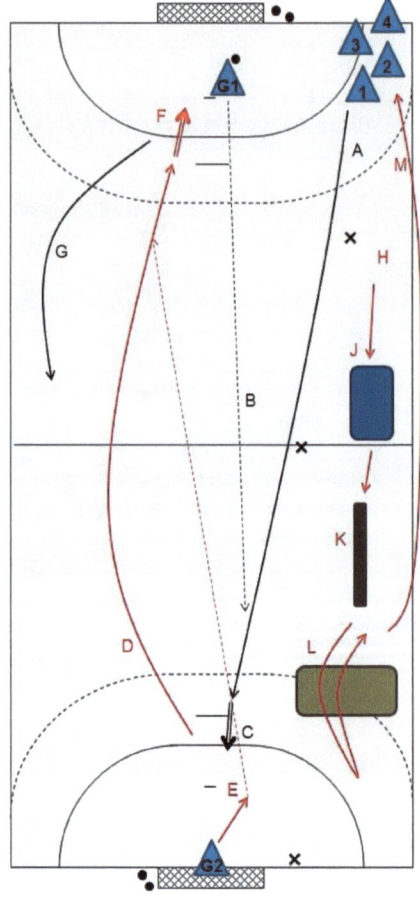

No. 67	Running with additional exercise on the large safety mat	8	★★★
	Topic:	Endurance	
	Equipment required:	6 cones, 2 large safety mats	

Setting:
- Position the cones (B and D) according to the players' level of performance.

Course:
- ① and ② start and do quick jumping jacks on the large safety mat (A).
- This is the sign for the other players to start. They sprint around the first cone (B), around the large safety mats (C), around the other cone (D), and back through the cone goal (E).
- Once the last player has run through the cone goal (E), ① and ② may stop doing jumping jacks.
- Repeat the course with the next two players on the large safety mats.
- Repeat until each player has done the course. Afterwards, the players may take a short break. Repeat the course 2 to 3 times, depending on the players' level of performance.

⚠ Adjust the distance of the backmost cones (B and D) to the team's level of performance.

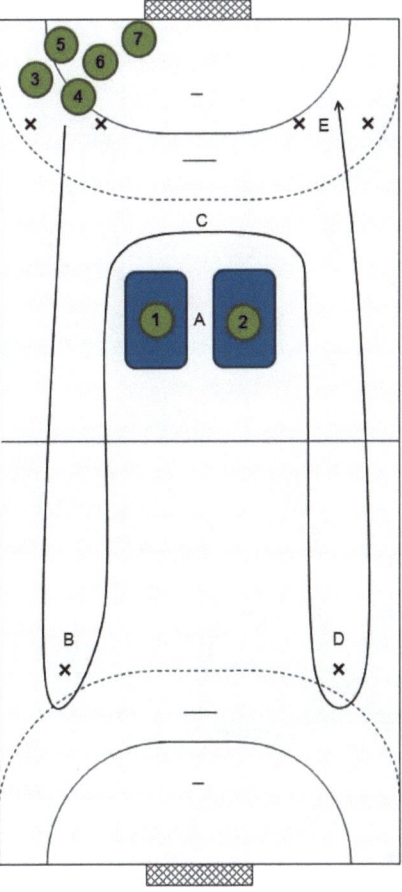

From warm-up to handball team play
75 exercises for every handball training

13. Example training unit

No.: 220	Shooting improvement and quick decision-making under pressure		★★	90
Opening part		**Main part**		
X	Warm-up/Stretching	X	Offense/Individual		Jumping power	
	Running exercise	X	Offense/Small groups		Sprint contest	
X	Short game		Offense/Team		Goalkeeper	
	Coordination	X	Offense/Series of shots			
	Coordination run		Defense/Individual		**Final part**	
	Strengthening		Defense/Small groups	X	Closing game	
	Ball familiarization		Defense/Team		Final sprint	
X	Goalkeeper warm-up shooting		Athletics			
			Endurance			

| ★ : Low level (all youth and adult teams) | ★ ★ : Medium level (youth teams under 15 years of age and adult teams) | ★ ★ ★ : High level (youth teams under 15 years of age and adult teams) | ★ ★ ★ ★ : Top level (competitive area) |

Key:

✗ Cone

▲ 1 Offense player

● 1 Defense player

⚫⚫⚫ Ball box

☐ Small vaulting box, upside-down

Equipment required:
→ 4 small vaulting boxes, 7 cones, 1 ball box with sufficient number of handballs

Description:
The objective of this training unit is to improve shooting and quick decision-making under pressure. During warm-up, the team must solve a task under time pressure. In a short game, the pressure increases due to additional external factors. After the goalkeeper warm-up shooting, a series of shots must be completed in combination with a brain-teaser. This is followed by an individual exercise, where the players must shoot under time pressure. Afterwards, there will be two exercises in small groups focusing on decision-making. The training unit is rounded off with a closing game.

The training unit consists of the following key exercises:
- Warm-up/Stretching (individual exercise: 10 minutes/total time: 10 minutes)
- Short game (10/20)
- Goalkeeper warm-up shooting (10/30)
- Offense/Series of shots (10/40)
- Offense/Individual (15/55)
- Offense/Small groups (10/65)
- Offense/Small groups (15/80)
- Closing game (10/90)

Training unit total time: 90 minutes

| No.: 220-1 | Warm-up/Stretching | 10 | 10 |

Course:
- The players crisscross throughout the entire half of the court. They have to do various running movements (running forward and backwards, sidestepping, hopping with forward and backward arm rotation, ...).
- The coach calls out a number between 3 and 5. The players now must form groups consisting of the respective number of players (coach calls out "4" → groups of 4) as fast as possible.
- The players who do not manage to get into a group must do an additional exercise (push-ups, squats, jumping jacks).
- Once the groups have formed, the coach sets a task. He calls out which and how many body parts may (and must) touch the floor. This applies to the whole group. The players receive a point when they solve the task first and manage to touch the floor with the correct body parts only. The groups must solve the task creatively (lift up one of the players, for example).
- Afterwards, the course starts over with the players crisscrossing throughout the half of the court.
- The three players who have the fewest points after 5 to 10 courses must do an additional exercise (carry the players with the most points on their back along the court, for example).

Examples for the group exercise:
- Teams of 3: 3 legs, 3 arms, 1 head
- Teams of 3: 2 legs, 4 arms
- Teams of 4: 4 legs, 2 arms, 1 head, 1 knee
- Teams of 4: 3 legs, 1 arm, 2 elbows
- Teams of 5: 4 legs, 2 arms, 2 knees, 2 elbows

| No.: 220-2 | Short game | 10 | 20 |

Setting:
- Put four small vaulting boxes upside down into the corners of the playing field.
- Make 2 teams; each team consists of 2 sub-teams (in the example: if you have 5 players per team, divide them into a sub-team of 2 and a sub-team of 3).

Overall course:
- The two sub-teams of 3 play against each other on a playing field between two vaulting boxes diagonal to each other. The two sub-teams of 2 play against each other on the playing field between the other vaulting boxes diagonal to each other.

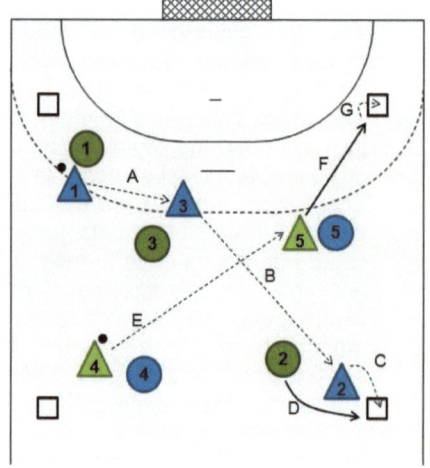

- At the end, the points of both sub-teams are added; this is the total score of the whole team.

- Which team scores highest?

Course:
- By playing quick passes (A, B, and E), the team in ball possession tries to position a player next to the opponents' box so that he can be passed to and lay the ball into the box (C and G). The team has scored then.
- Once the ball is in the box, the defending team secures the ball (D) and starts a counter attack on the opponents' box.
- When playing 2-on-2, the players may dribble (F).

⚠ Since the teams play 3-on-3 and 2-on-2 on diagonal playing fields at the same time, the players must keep in mind that there will be some traffic when playing the individual actions. The players must approach the opponents' box, but also pay attention to the other teams crossing their field diagonally.

⚠ If there are more players or fewer players per team, split the teams accordingly (2 times 3-on-3; 2 times 2-on-2).

| No.: 220-3 | Goalkeeper warm-up shooting | 10 | 30 |

Setting:
- Position cones for a slalom run as shown in the figure.
- Divide the team into two groups. One group begins with shooting at the goal, the other one with the slalom run.

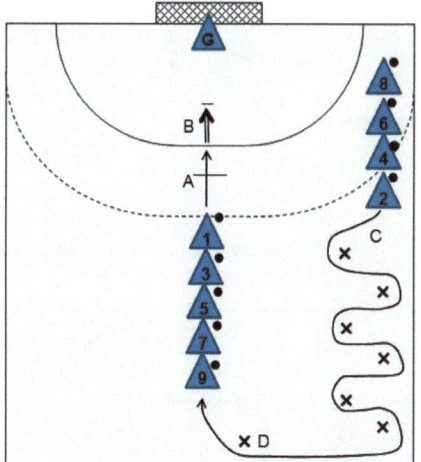

Course:
-  starts with a ball (A), shoots as instructed (hands, top, bottom) (B), lines up with the ball behind 8, and starts the slalom run after 8.
- 3 starts the same course immediately afterwards, etc.
- 2 starts at the same time as 1, does the slalom run through the cones as instructed (C), then runs around the backmost cone (D), and lines up behind 9. 2 shoots after 9.
- As soon as 2 has arrived the third cone, 4 starts the slalom run.
- Once each player has shot, the groups line up again and the course starts over with the next shooting instruction.

⚠ The players should time their shots in such a way that they maintain a regular rhythm for the goalkeeper.

Slalom instructions:
- Run forward and dribble with the right (left) hand.
- Sidestep and move the handball around your hips in circles.
- Sidestep and dribble.

| No.: 220-4 | Offense/Series of shots | 10 | 40 |

Setting:
- Position cones for a slalom run as shown in the figure.

Course:

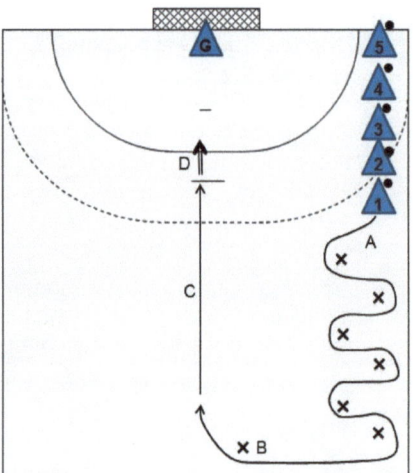

- 1 starts with a ball and does a slalom run around the cones as instructed (forward or sidestepping while dribbling with the left and right hand alternately) (A).
- Afterwards, 1 runs around the cone (B), starts running towards the goal (C), and eventually shoots at the goal (D).
- While 1 is running towards the goal, the coach calls out numbers (7, 5, 12, for example).
- Immediately after 1 has shot, he must call out the sum of the numbers the coach has called out.
- Once 1 has finished the slalom run, 2 starts the same course.

⚠ The players should concentrate on their shot at the goal in spite of the brain-teaser.

| No.: 220-5 | Offense/Individual | 15 | 55 |

Setting:
- Position cones as shown in the figure.

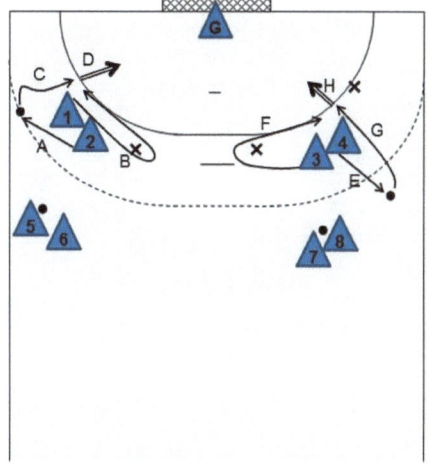

Course:
- The exercise is done on the left wing and the right back position alternately. Change the sides after several courses (right wing and left back).
- The players form pairs (change pairs during each course).
- The first pair puts their ball on the floor on the 9-meter line on the wing position. The players stand face-to-face between the 6- and 9-meter line and hold hands. One player is assigned the color "black", the other one the color "white".
- The coach calls out "black" or "white".
- The respective player (here 2) runs towards the ball (A), picks it up, and approaches the goal (C).
- The other player (1) runs around the cone (B) and tries to and tries to slightly interfere with the shot of the first player (D).
- In the meantime, the first pair on the right back position has put their ball on the floor in front of the 9-meter line and chosen their colors, "black" or "white".
- Once again, the coach calls out "black" or "white", the respective player (4) fetches the ball (E), approaches the goal (G), and shoots (H). The other player (3) runs around the cone (F), confines the space for the attacking player's break-through, and slightly interferes with the shot.
- Afterwards, the next pair starts on the left wing position, etc.

⚠ In spite of the time pressure and the defending player's action, the attacking players should approach the goal at full speed, jump, and concentrate on the shot.

Variant:
- Instead of calling out "black" or "white", the coach calls out a word that is associated with the respective color (e.g., milk, cloud, coal, night, ...).

| No.: 220-6 | Offense/Small groups | 10 | 65 |

Setting:
- Position two cones on the left and right side of the 7-meter line. Define the playing field with two other cones.

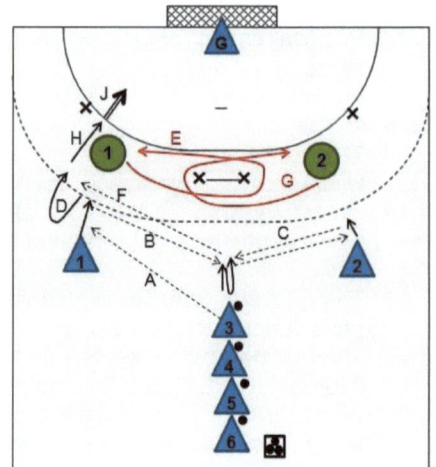

Course:
- 3 passes the ball and starts the game (A).
- 1 makes a piston movement and passes back to 3 (B) who passes to 2 (C).
- Once 1 has played the pass (B), 1 runs around the furthermost cone on the 7-meter line (E).
- The ball is being passed back from 2 to 3 to 1 (F) who has slightly moved back and now makes a new piston movement (D).
- 1 must now make a decision:
    o If 1 has moved back to his defense position in time, 1 passes back to 3.
    o If 1 has been too slow, 1 breaks through (H) and shoots (J).
- Once 2 has played the pass, 2 also runs around the furthermost cone on the 7-meter line (G).
- 1, 2, and 3 make the piston movement and keep passing on the back positions until 1 or 2 can break through.
- The player who has shot lines up in the center with a ball again; 3 takes over his position and 4 starts over the course from the center back position.

⚠ The players must run a wide piston movement path and play proper passes in order to prepare a break-through.

⚠ The exercise is very exhausting for the defense players; therefore, change the players regularly.

⚠ After about 2 to 3 piston movements, a break-through should be possible. Increase/decrease the distance for the defense players by changing the position of the inner cones accordingly. If the attacking players cannot break through, make the defensive players' situation more challenging (the defensive players must touch the floor with both hands/sit down, for example, before they may start to run around the cones).

| No.: 220-7 | Offense/Individual | 15 | 80 |

Setting:
- Position two cones on the left and right side of the 7-meter line.

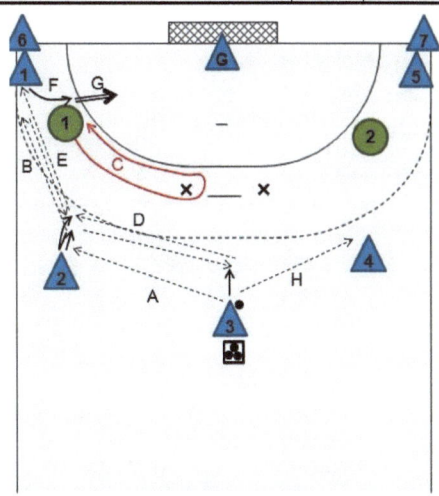

Course:
- 3 initially starts the course to the left (A).
- 3 passes the ball to 2 who passes the ball to the wing player (1) who passes back (A and B).
- Once 1 passes back to 2, 1 runs around the cone at the 7-meter line (C).
- Once the ball comes back from 3 and 2 (D) to 1 (E), 1 must make a decision:
    o If 1 has moved back to his defense position in time, 1 passes back to 2.
    o If 1 has been too slow, 1 breaks through (F) and shoots from the wing position (G).
- 1, 2, and 3 make the piston movement and pass the ball until 1 manages to break through and shoot.
- Afterwards, 3 takes a new ball from the ball box and starts the course to the right with 4 and 5, and 2 playing defense.

⚠ The exercise is very exhausting for the defense players; therefore, change the players regularly.

⚠ After about 2 to 3 passes to the wing player, a break through should be possible. If the attacking players cannot break through, make the defensive players' situation more challenging (the defensive players must touch the floor with both hands/sit down, for example, before they may start to run around the cones).

No.: 220-8	Closing game		10	90

Course:
- Make two teams.
- The first team starts playing offense and plays an attack against 2 defense players (A, B, and C).
- If they score a goal, the next attack must be played against three defense players (D).
- If they do not score a goal, the next attack will be played against the same number of defense players as before.
- If they lose the ball due to a technical mistake or if the defense players steal the ball, one of the defense players leaves the playing field.

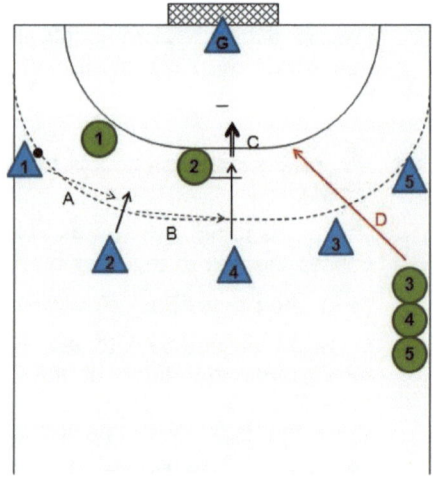

- The attacking players try to score a goal as fast as possible while there is an even number of defense players on the playing field. Measure the time and switch tasks afterwards.
- Which team scores faster when there is an even number of defense players?
- If a team is not able to fulfill the task within 5 minutes, switch tasks and write down the number of defense players on the playing field at the time of discontinuation.

Variants:
- Instead of measuring the time, you may also count the number of attacks needed to fulfill the task.

 The team must fetch the ball themselves – the time keeps running.

JÖRG MADINGER, born in Heidelberg (Germany) in 1970

July 2014 (further training): 3-day coaching workshop: "Basic components of goalkeeper training", held by the German Handball Association (Deutscher Handballbund, DHB)
Lecturers: Michael Neuhaus, Renate Schubert, Marco Stange, Norbert Potthoff, Olaf Gritz, Andreas Thiel, Henning Fritz

May 2014 (further training): 3-day coaching further training during the VELUX EHF Final4, held by the **German Handball Coaching Association (Deutsche Handball Trainer Vereinigung, DHTV)/DHB**
Lecturers: Jochen Beppler (DHB coach), Christian vom Dorff (DHB referee), Mark Dragunski (coach of TuSeM Essen, Germany),
Klaus-Dieter Petersen (DHB coach), Manolo Cadenas (coach of the Spanish national team)

May 2013 (further training): 3-day coaching further training during the VELUX EHF Final4, held by the **German Handball Coaching Association (Deutsche Handball Trainer Vereinigung, DHTV)/DHB**
Lecturers: Prof. Dr. Carmen Borggrefe (University of Stuttgart, Germany), Klaus-Dieter Petersen (DHB coach), Dr. Georg Froese (sports psychologist), Jochen Beppler (DHB base camp coach), Carsten Alisch (young talents' hockey coach)

Since July 2012: A-License, DHB

Since February 2011: Handball club trainings, coaching (training and competitive areas)

November 2011: Foundation of the Handball Specialist Publishing Company (Handball Fachverlag) (handall-uebungen.de, Handball Practice and Special Handball Practice)

May 2009: Foundation of the handball online platform handball-uebungen.de

2008-2010: Youth coordinator and youth coach, SG Leutershausen (Germany)

Since 2006: B-License

Editor's note

In 1995, a friend convinced me to join him in coaching a handball youth team (male, under 13 years of age).

This was the beginning of my career as a team handball coach. Ever since I enjoyed working as a coach and had high requirements concerning my exercises. Soon, the standard pool of exercises wasn't enough for me anymore and I started to modify and develop drills myself.

Today, I coach a broad range of youth and adult teams with different performance levels and adjust my training units to the individual needs of the teams.

A few years ago, I started selling my exercises and drills online at handball-uebungen.de. Since, in handball training, there is a tendency towards a general athletic training that focuses on coordination work – especially in the training of youth teams –, a large number of my games and exercises can be applied to other sports as well.

Get inspired by the various game concepts, be creative, and rely on your own experiences!

Yours sincerely,
Jörg Madinger

www.ingramcontent.com/pod-product-compliance
Lightning Source LLC
Chambersburg PA
CBHW041802160426
43191CB00001B/14